GETTING BACK TO THE BASICS OF PUBLIC RELATIONS & PUBLICITY

GETTING BACK TO THE BASICS OF PUBLIC RELATIONS & PUBLICITY

Matthew J. Culligan and Dolph Greene

CROWN PUBLISHERS, INC.
NEW YORK

Published by Crown Publishers, Inc., One Park Avenue, New York, New York 10016, and simultaneously in Canada by General Publishing Company Limited

Manufactured in the United States of America

Library of Congress Cataloging in Publication Data

Culligan, Matthew J., 1918–
    Getting back to the basics of public relations and publicity.

    Bibliography: p.
    Includes index.
    1. Public relations.   2. Publicity.   I. Greene, Dolph. II. Title.
HM263.C75   1982   659.2   82-9935
ISBN:0-517-54722-8   AACR2

10 9 8 7 6 5 4 3 2 1

First Edition

To the Public Relations Society of America, whose officers and members have, through the years, given of their time, effort, and intellect to establish public relations as a socially responsible profession.

The PRSA's library, publications, classes, meetings, and policing activities have been instrumental in achieving for our craft the position it now enjoys in corporate boardrooms, halls of government, institutions of learning, and in most other centers of contemporary life.

Public sentiment is everything. . . . With public sentiment nothing can fail. Without it, nothing can succeed. He who molds public sentiment goes deeper than he who executes statutes or pronounces decisions. He makes statutes or decisions possible or impossible to execute.

ABRAHAM LINCOLN

ACKNOWLEDGMENTS

—

The authors are deeply indebted to Robert McLaren, now an independent financial-relations consultant in New York City, for his insistence that we stop talking about this book and sit down to write it. We are grateful, also, for the information he supplied for the Denim Council case history; to James W. Thompson, director of corporate public relations and advertising of National Gypsum Company, for his encouragement and the facts upon which the National Gypsum case history is based; to Sam Tyndall and Ginal Calkins of Samuel S. Tyndall Associates in St. Petersburg, Florida, for their enthusiasm and effort in digging up the records of the Houze Glass Company program; to Denny Griswold and Jack O'Dwyer and the other journalists who service the public-relations profession for informing us, criticizing us when we needed it, and applauding us when we warranted it; to the public-relations practitioners, clients, and media people with whom we have worked over the years—we learned from each of them. They, in a very real sense, are the authors of this book.

CONTENTS

═══

Contents

PREFACE

This book will not promise you a rose garden. Public relations is a hard, exacting craft. It has its share of disappointments and frustrations. I remember a colleague's insistence that "this would be a great business if it weren't for the clients, the media people, and the public."

Despite the problems inherent in any field, public relations provides many satisfactions and rewards. It has been my profession for more than twenty-five years. It has paid the rent, put food on the table, and permitted me more than a few very pleasant extras.

Beyond these things, it has given me some great satisfactions. I have been exposed to industries, professions, disciplines, whole bodies of knowledge that otherwise would have been foreign to me. I got paid for minding other people's business.

I knew nothing about computer software, for instance, until the agency for which I worked was retained by a company in that business. I received a crash course in the industry and was paid while I took it. I will never be an expert, of course. I will never know as much about it as the client I represented, but I understood what he was talking about. I can read an article on new developments with some comprehension.

Throughout a normal public-relations career such opportunities are frequent, and painlessly, you find yourself becoming much better educated, a more interested and interesting human being.

There is an old folk song, "Newspapermen Meet Such Interesting People." So do public-relations professionals: media people, heads of companies both big and small, scientists, economists, visionaries with dreams for new products or services, writers, art-ists—people in almost all professions with divergent ways of life.

Over the years you learn to heed Shakespeare's advice not to "dull your palm with entertainment of each new-hatched, un-fledged comrade," but with certain few contacts who become friends to "grapple . . . to thy soul with hoops of steel." If, during your lifetime, you make one or two good friends because of the way you earn your living, it is a magnificent plus.

All this is the long way around to how this book was born. It had a longer gestation period than a baby elephant. In 1963, while I was vice-president of Robert S. Taplinger Associates, a public-relations agency, we were retained to represent the Curtis Publishing Company, publishers of the *Saturday Evening Post.* Curtis had been in deep trouble brought on by internal power struggles and serious financial losses. Matthew J. Culligan had just been appointed president of the company and was charged with the responsibility of getting Curtis back on its feet. I had never met Joe Culligan but I had heard of him. Everyone in the commu-nications industry had. His contributions to the success of the National Broadcasting Company (he had been president of NBC Radio and executive vice-president of NBC TV) were legendary. His name automatically came to mind at the mention of such shows as "Today" and "Tonight."

After he had left NBC but before he had joined Curtis, Joe had been the general corporate executive and director of Interpublic, Inc., one of the largest advertising agencies in the world.

As I began to learn about the magazine publishing business, I watched Joe in action. In the space of one year he reorganized, restaffed, and refinanced that faltering company and brought it back to profitability, reducing the annual loss by $15 million. And through all this activity, which earned him a citation by the *New York Times* as one of the "executives who left a strong imprint on American business," he never lost his public-relations sense. He constantly kept open his lines of communication with all Curtis's various publics—its readers, advertisers, employees, and share-holders.

This awareness of public relations was extremely important when, in 1964, a group of "raiders" started a hostile takeover of the company that Joe had made profitable. A proxy battle was underway. Curtis Publishing, aided by our agency, won the fight.

And that year, Matthew J. Culligan and Robert S. Taplinger Associates won the Public Relations Society of America's prestigious Silver Anvil award for "the corporate public-relations program that worked."

I was sitting next to Bob McLaren, Taplinger's president, during the awards dinner in New York when Joe accepted the statuette.

"There," I said to Bob, "is one man who should write a book on public relations. He has made it work for him consistently."

"Don't tell me," Bob said, "tell him."

I did tell him—but not until some sixteen years later. Joe suggested that, as we had worked at public relations from two different approaches, we write the book together.

We realize that there are already many books in print on this subject. Why yet another? Because too many of these works are "pie-in-the-sky" theoretical excursions that have little to do with the men and women who make their living in public relations or those who wish to enter that field. Like so many others on the American business scene, our industry tends to get too complicated and oversophisticated and forgets its basic functions.

It is time to restate those basics and to get back to them. This book attempts to do just that.

DOLPH GREENE

FOREWORD

Public Relations is at least as old as the United States. Alexander Hamilton and James Monroe practiced it intuitively, yet professionally, when they presented the Constitution for the people's ratification.

They evaluated public attitudes, spelled out policies and procedures in the people's best interests, and earned public understanding and acceptance for a revolutionary form of government that has stood steadfast against the tests of time, strife, economic disorder, and social upheaval.

It does not matter that Hamilton and Monroe had never heard of public relations—or were unaware they were practicing it—as they analyzed, organized, and visualized the situations of their day.

It matters even less that Joe Culligan's respected reputation was built as a salesman and corporate executive, since his collaborator, Dolph Greene, brings more than thirty years of public-relations experience to the project. Their *Getting Back to the Basics of Public Relations and Publicity* is intuitive as well as professional.

The book tweaks the executive intellect and jogs the memory sufficiently to recall to the mind of anyone responsible for directing or changing public perception of the ABCs of the business.

When sound public relations is used creatively, it touches every phase of the operation of a corporation, industry, or institution. It also relates to the man in the street and just about everyone else.

Joe Culligan and Dolph Greene remind us that the basics of sound public relations can stimulate a fresh perspective that is always healthy. They must have had one hand on the pulse of the public-relations profession and the other on the keyboard of their typewriters when they poured their thoughts into this book with nary a bit of semantic nonsense. Their research, planning, execution, and evaluation—generally recognized steps in professional PR development—are faultless. They are right on target with respect to such areas as the financial community, marketing support, employee and community relations, and in areas of government, labor, and other public relations that are of interest to everyone.

February 1, 1982

ROBERT J. WOOD
President,
Carl Byoir & Associates, Inc.

—1—

WHAT IS PUBLIC RELATIONS?

Public relations is the total communications effort of a person, a company, an agency, a group, a government, or any organization to its various publics.

There are as many definitions of public relations as there are people who follow the craft. Almost everyone has a version and most of them are incomplete. Perhaps, then, it might be profitable to start by outlining what public relations is not.

PUBLIC RELATIONS IS NOT ADVERTISING. Although this is one of the most prevalent misconceptions about the field, it often uses advertising as a tool; in fact, a public-relations campaign is almost always coordinated with an advertising program. But it is not "paid-for" space and time that you buy in newspapers, magazines, on radio or television.

PUBLIC RELATIONS IS NOT PUBLICITY. It is not getting your name in the paper or on radio or television. Publicity is generally an important and essential element of public relations, but it is always just one part of the whole. It is true, however, that getting unpaid editorial space or time in the media is a primary objective of most public-relations programs, for reasons that will be discussed later in this book.

PUBLIC RELATIONS IS NOT SALES PROMOTION, POINT-OF-SALE DISPLAYS, CONTESTS, SPEECHES, PERSONAL APPEARANCES, MEMBERSHIP IN ORGANIZATIONS, or, for that matter, any single isolated thing. A public-relations program involves all these and more, but it is larger than the sum of its parts. These are some of the tools that public relations uses, but they do not define the general term. What, then, is public relations?

When a customer deals with any member of your organization and is satisfied, that is good public relations. When your appearance and knowledge make a favorable impression on anyone in your community or in your industry or in the media, that is good

1

public relations. When you contribute your time and effort to a worthy cause, that is good public relations. In short, any contact you have with another human being is part of public relations—your personal total communications effort.

The purpose of this book is to suggest ways that a communications program can be made more effective; ways in which you can better use tools and opportunities now at your disposal and develop new ones; and ways in which your individual activities can reinforce the entire program of your company or organization.

MANY PUBLICS

Any person or organization planning a public-relations program must analyze the various "publics" upon which it depends and that it must influence.

For the purposes of this book, we will presume that you are a line public-relations executive for a division of a publicly held company that has a corporate public-relations department with which you can cooperate. The principles and techniques we discuss should have validity for you no matter what your specific situation.

Who are the publics of such a publicly held company that manufactures products for industrial and/or consumer use? To what groups must we direct our communications? There are many:

THE ULTIMATE CONSUMERS

How do they break down demographically in terms of age, sex, income level, geographic location, and so forth? You must identify your public before you can design a program to reach it. Appealing to the teenage market with a product for senior citizens would be pointless. It might be possible to sell refrigerators to Eskimos, but there are easier ways to make a living.

THE SHAREHOLDERS

If you expect your company's securities to enjoy a good market, you must certainly keep the holders of those securities informed and confident. How many stockholders are there? Where do they live? How many shares of stock do they own? All these factors will influence the ways in which they might best be approached.

THE INVESTMENT COMMUNITY

This includes security analysts, brokers, bankers, investment bankers, and so on. These people must be familiar with the company and its management so they can support it in the marketplace and recommend it as a sound corporation.

THE PRIMARY CONSUMER

These are the wholesalers, retailers, jobbers, builders, and others who are the primary customers for the company's products and who make the initial purchase. The ultimate consumer will never see these products unless the "middlemen" are confident of their profitability and reliability.

THE COMMUNITIES

The communities are those in which the company has factories, offices, or other installations. A reputation as a good corporate citizen is vital to the well-being of any firm. Opposition from misinformed special-interest groups, local officials, or other concerned citizens can be a major problem. Open, effective communication is crucial for developing a mutual understanding of the needs and goals of both the company and the communities in which it operates.

THE COMPANY'S SUPPLIERS

They are important to the company's existence. Building mutual trust and a feeling of interdependence with your company's suppliers is essential for a smooth, profitable business life.

THE MEDIA AND OTHER OPINION MOLDERS

The various media must be prime targets of any complete public-relations effort, for they are the conduit through which the company's story will flow to all its other publics. They require—and deserve—intensive cultivation and attention.

GOVERNMENT AGENCIES

Government bodies on all levels—federal, state, and local—must be sympathetic to the company's goals and activities, because, whether we like it or not, they can have a profound influence on the firm's success.

THE GENERAL PUBLIC

This large, nebulous, indefinable mass includes all the above. It involves the complete environment in which the company exists. Ultimately, the general public holds in its hands the power to determine the success or failure of the company. It is the master.

These are some of the publics to which our fictitious company must tailor its public-relations program.

The next logical question: Why bother? Why must any company communicate with these publics? Why can't it just go about its business and ignore them? It can, of course. Thousands of bankrupt companies attest to this possibility.

WHY IS THERE A NEED FOR PUBLIC RELATIONS AND WHAT DOES IT ACCOMPLISH?

An essential step in creating a public-relations program, then, is the clarification of objectives. In other words, what does a company hope to accomplish through this effort?

1. To improve sales. This is a prerequisite for a healthy company.
2. To increase earnings. Companies are in business to make money. (There are other reasons, but this one is primary and basic to corporate existence.)
3. To broaden the base of ownership of the company's securities and to assure the proper valuation in the marketplace. The shareholder and the financial community as a whole will support excellent performance if they are told about it clearly and professionally.

There are many barometers used to measure the effectiveness of public relations and publicity. The price of a public company's securities on either of the major stock exchanges ranks very high on this list. Corporate managements have risen and fallen with stock prices or price-earnings ratios.

One pointed example is in the field of commercial broadcasting in the P/E ratio game. The RCA stock is a composite of the earnings of many divisions of this gigantic corporation. However, when NBC, which is owned by RCA, slipped from first place in the television network ratings into second, the RCA stock price was inordinately affected. When NBC slipped further, into third place, the RCA stock dipped again in actual value and its P/E ratio dropped as well.

So, stockholder and financial-community relations must command the attention of the public-relations and publicity practitioner.

4. To convey the company's message to the community. This is particularly important since the community can have an impact in the critical areas of environment, employment, taxes, and so forth.
5. To secure for the company a respected position in its parent industry. People enjoy doing business with a "winner." Since this program is built on performance, the public-relations story must convey the company's expertise, past successes, future potential, and general strength and reliability.
6. To establish, maintain, and constantly reinforce the company's relationship with all segments of the media. Defining publics, determining objectives, and deciding how best to tell the story are all basic to the program. However, they accomplish nothing by themselves. They must be translated into action. The predetermined messages must be conveyed to the selected audiences to achieve the desired objectives. The media are of primary importance in accomplishing this task.

2

THE ELEMENTS OF A
PUBLIC-RELATIONS PROGRAM:
THE MEDIA

We have established in Chapter 1 the importance of the media in any public-relations effort. In this chapter we will discuss the elements of a public-relations program, focusing on the media, both print and electronic, and on the all-important press conference.

ADVERTISING

Advertising offers several advantages. It tells the company's story directly and in precisely the way that is desired. The advertiser, within certain limitations imposed by law and good taste, has complete control of content. And, since space is purchased, the message always appears at the desired time and in the chosen media.

Advertising does, however, have two major limitations: it is expensive, which tends to inhibit its use; and no matter how well it is put together, it bears the stigma of self-interest. The most naive of readers, viewers, or listeners is aware that an ad is telling the story from the point of view of the advertiser. It is impossible to claim objectivity.

This is not meant to denigrate the effectiveness of advertising. Its success stories are too numerous. But it is important to recognize the limitations of our tools so that they can be used for the greatest effect.

PUBLICITY AND MEDIA RELATIONS

Publicity is any print space or air time that the company obtains in the editorial segment of the media without payment. Publicity is valuable, of course, only if it reflects favorably on the company and is consistent with its self-image. The old adage "I don't care what they say about me as long as they spell my name right" still might be valid for circus performers and politicians, but it is long out of date for business organizations.

Knowing your local media people will not guarantee you a story if your material doesn't warrant one. If they are good reporters—and many are—nothing will do that. But establishing a consistent relationship with local media, based on reliability and truthfulness, will assure that your ideas get a fair hearing. Many reporters and editors, once they come to rely on you and trust you, may suggest that a story might interest them if you could develop another approach. When this happens, you know you have established excellent media relations.

These suggestions are important, but there are two hard and fast interrelated principles that must never be violated when you are dealing with the media. They are:

Always tell the truth.
Never say anything to a media person, anywhere, at any time,
on any subject that is "off the record."

The first principle appears to be simple, but sometimes it is not. If you are not authorized to impart certain information, admit it. If, for example, you are asked a question concerning corporate policy or finances, do not give the classic "no comment" answer that newspeople hate. Inform them that it does not fall into your area and that you will have someone from corporate public relations call them. If you are asked an esoteric question in your own field that you cannot answer, again, admit it. However, assure the reporter that you will be happy to get the requested information and, of course, do so.

As for the second principle, this applies no matter how close a friend or good a contact the media representative is. Telling a reporter something "off the record" puts him or her in an uncomfortable position of conflict between loyalty to you and the con-

cept of the public's "right to know." If you don't want to see it in
print or hear it on the air, don't say it.

A NOSE FOR NEWS

We cannot proceed to the more detailed discussion of the media
without considering the need for developing the ability to recognize news, the basis of much of the public-relations effort.

Newsworthy events occur in any organization. The big stories
are obvious: a major change affecting many people, a new discov-
ery, an expansion plan, the construction of a plant—activities such
as these deserve public attention. But these are not the only newsworthy items. Many a news story has been published because an
alert executive recognized its worth when no one else in the organization was aware of its interest or timeliness.

You must constantly look for news. You must develop a sense
of what news is and which media will use it. You must be aware
that an item might be old to you and to your organization but
new to the readers of some publication.

Consider the following: More than 1 million corporate news
stories produced by sixteen billion-dollar companies were analyzed by computer and broken down by categories as follows:

34.5%—product publicity
28.9%—"growth" stories (increased earnings and sales, merger
       and acquisitions, expansion, and so forth)
 7.8%—general marketing activity
 7.6%—corporate social concern
 2.8%—negative news (sales and earnings off, strikes,
       employment down, and so forth)

This leaves a little less than 19 percent for miscellaneous stories. Your company will get its fair share of the first four categories if you function properly. The additional space, almost 19
percent, is up for grabs. It must be obtained with your imagination and your ability to communicate. Your ability to find the
news will get your company a piece of that space.

Remember, if you think something is a story, then it may well be. If you think you have a great idea, you just may have one. Be a mental miser. Throw away nothing that is in any way creative.

A GENERAL SURVEY OF THE MEDIA

Dealing with the media is a complex subject. The first, and most important, step is to identify the media that will be targeted by your program. If you do not already have them, prepare lists of:

THE DAILY PRESS

List all the dailies in your "affect community." ° This may include papers in neighboring cities and states and, conceivably, as far afield as New York, Chicago, and Los Angeles, if your activities affect those areas. Having the addresses of newspapers is not enough. You should list the names of business editors, reporters covering your industry, new-products people, and others who might be interested in news from your company. Directing your material to the right person has a lot to do with whether or not it will be used. This may seem a monumental task, but, really, it is not. Usually, one phone call to each paper will accomplish your purpose. Remember, newspapers need your material and generally will cooperate to see that it reaches the correct person. Before you make your call, write out your questions. When you call the paper, identify yourself and your company and indicate the kind of information you require. When you are asking questions about the source, be brief and concise. After you get your information, if the person on the other end seems interested, discuss your needs with him or her but be aware of the limits on the time of a working newspaper person. Try to avoid calling when the reporters are on a deadline. For morning newspapers, the deadline is usually late afternoon of the previous day for the early editions, and early evening for the final editions. With afternoon papers, the deadline is generally early evening of the previous day for the first editions and later in the night of the previous day

° See Chapter 5, page 41, for definition of "affect community."

or early in the morning of the same day for finals. These dead-lines apply to the kind of material you will usually supply. Late-breaking, immediately important hard news will be accepted whenever it comes in. These are general rules. You will have to obtain the specific deadlines of the papers you contact.

THE WIRE SERVICES

These are the two giant wires that supply news to thousands of newspapers, electronic media, and publications throughout the world. Start by finding out if there are AP (Associated Press) and UPI (United Press International) bureaus in your city. If not, the bureau in the nearest larger city will usually be responsible for covering your unit's activities. Call and get the name of the person to contact should the need arise. You will discover that except for the major bureaus (New York, Washington, D.C., Chicago, and so forth), there is less departmentalization on the wire services than in the daily press. Your AP list, for example, might consist of just one person to whom all material should be sent.

THE BUSINESS NEWS WIRES

The Dow-Jones and Reuters financial news wires are interested primarily in business news. Their wires go to investment houses, brokerages, banks, and other members of the financial community as well as to media. Generally, contact with them will be re-stricted to corporate public relations, if your company has such a department, but there might be times when you wish to contact them, with the approval of your corporate office. Once again, use the telephone to determine the bureau nearest you and the person or persons most interested in your material.

TRADE PAPERS AND MAGAZINES

In preparing your list of trade publications, it is important to remember that what your customer or potential customer reads is more important to you than what you yourself may prefer to read. This list should include the publications of your own industry, of course, but it should also contain the papers and magazines of your customers' businesses. For instance, if you sell to the auto-repair industry, its publications should be on the list. Just about every industry—from hardware, do-it-yourself, interior decorating, home repair and remodeling, office supply and design, to any one of dozens of other industries—has one or more trade publications. Analyze the customer and potential customer lists you will draw up in Chapter 7, and from them create your trade-publications master list. Structure the list for use in whole or in part, as the news warrants.

THE ELECTRONIC MEDIA

The late Marshall McLuhan became rich by writing books that proclaimed that nobody reads anymore. While this is an extreme claim, it is true that television and radio have certainly become a vital element of any communications program. Incorporating them into the program can be a complicated process. The first step, however, is locating them in your area.

Begin with the local affiliates of the three major networks. While you may seldom have news or features of interest to a national network, these channels and stations function, much of the time, as local outlets. Add to this list the independent television (including cable) and radio stations. Their "call letters" can be found in your area's telephone directories. Use the phone, once again, to find out the names of the assignment editors, news editors, and producers of local interview and talk shows. There will be additional broadcasters you will want to contact with specific stories, but your basic electronic-media list will include these people.

Realistically, the proliferation of radio stations and the differences in the organization of various television channels might make these lists more difficult to assemble. There are, however, excellent reference directories available.

MAGAZINES

General-interest national magazines are usually either staff written or will accept contributions only from well-known free-lance writers or from literary agents. For the most part they will not consider unsolicited material but will, occasionally, follow up on ideas suggested to them. When you think that you might have such a story, attempt to develop specific approaches suitable for a particular publication. Regional and special-interest books will sometimes accept contributed material. To the greatest extent possible, familiarize yourself with those in your "affect community" area and with those interested in your field of activity.

The news-gathering structure of news magazines such as *Time, Newsweek, U.S. News & World Report,* and others is very much like that of a major daily newspaper. These weeklies have offices in principal cities around the nation. Find out where their closest offices are. While all their material is staff written, they do appreciate tips, leads, or story ideas and frequently seek help from organizations involved in the field with which their story is concerned. In addition to the address of the magazine, list the editor or reporters who cover your business.

WEEKLIES, SHOPPERS, CLUB PAPERS

Wherever you live and do business there are weekly newspapers and "shoppers." The latter are mainly advertising vehicles for local merchants. These papers, of course, have much smaller readerships than dailies, but they are often loyal readerships with money to spend. These papers are usually hungry for material. Since you are interested in results, not prestige, they deserve your attention.

Use the Yellow Pages in your area to draw up a list of these publications, and find out the names of the editors. In most cases, he or she will be the reporter as well, and therefore, the correct contact for any kind of story.

Many organizations in your community will also produce their own publications, and many of them use general-interest material. Large corporations with external publications, church groups, fraternal organizations, men's and women's clubs, and many other organizations may offer possibilities for placing stories. Get as many of these as you can from the Yellow Pages and other sources.

FEATURE SERVICES

On a smaller scale than AP and UPI there are a number of services that distribute feature material to publications throughout the country. They may be useful to you since they are not interested in hard news but are receptive to "how-to," human-interest, industry-trend, and changing life-style stories. Since these services are national, lists of them are available in publicity directories.

Over the years, different service organizations have grown up to aid in the placement of material in the media. These include:

Public-Relations News Wires
They teletype your material to newspapers, radio and television stations, trade magazines, and press associations, using their own leased wires.

Mat Services (or feature syndicates or news and picture services)
They will put your stories and pictures on mats for reproduction onto letterpress or "slicks" for offset use, and distribute them to an agreed-upon number of publications.

Public-Relations Mailing Houses
They will send your material to general or specialized lists in categories that you select.

All these services, and some that we have not listed, have one thing in common—they charge a fee. We would suggest, generally, that you avoid using them simply because we believe you can do the job better yourself for less money. There might, however, be specific situations where time or other factors indicate that using one of these aids might be advantageous. Such services are usually listed in the Yellow Pages and will be happy to send you price lists and other information.

Taken together, all the above elements make up your media public.

Now it is important to discuss methods and techniques for using the various media sectors that we have identified and that you have listed.

THE DAILY PRESS

There will be two general categories of material you will be distributing to your daily-press list:

HARD NEWS

Such information as appointments, openings, moves, new products, plant expansions, and so forth is not exclusive. That is, you are not promising any publication that it will have the story to the exclusion of all others. These releases should be distributed to your entire media list. However, when sending material to more than one person on the same publication, note on the release the names of others who have received it, to avoid confusion.

You should attempt to establish a distribution schedule which ensures that all publications receive the release simultaneously, taking into account deadlines and time for delivery.

Generally speaking, it is preferable to distribute news releases on Monday, Tuesday, or Wednesday, since this gives the editor the option, if he receives it on a heavy news day, of holding the material without running into the weekend.

(For a discussion and examples of writing hard-news releases, see Chapter 3.)

FEATURES

For our purposes, we designate all stories that are not hard news as features. This also includes editorial interviews, with which we will deal in a separate section.

Every publication offers innumerable opportunities for feature placement. You should read and understand the specific needs and areas of interest, not only of each publication but also of any of its departments that may relate to your program.

If, for example, your company manufactures building products, then the real-estate editor, the financial and business departments, the editors and reporters responsible for construction, science, the environment, how-to stories, and general features might all be markets for stories you have to sell—each from a different point of view.

You may not be a skilled writer. You probably do not have professional newspaper experience, but you will not need it, since most papers are mainly staff-written. Instead, you are going to suggest the idea, offer to provide the background material, and aid the reporter in putting the story together.

Experience has demonstrated that the best way to do this is

through a "pitch letter" to the appropriate editor. This letter should outline the story you are suggesting, list the background material you have available, the names of people you can provide for interviews, and all other pertinent material. (For a more detailed discussion of pitch letters, and some examples, see Chapter 4.)

Give the editor a reasonable length of time to consider your suggestion—two or three days—and then call to discuss it. If he tells you he is considering the story, ask when you might call again. *Do not become a pest.* Do not invent reasons to call.

A feature suggestion is exclusive. This means that you are promising the editor you will suggest the story to no one else until you hear from him. After a reasonable length of time—perhaps a week—it is perfectly logical for you to call and request a final decision. If he rejects the idea, you are, of course, free to send your story idea elsewhere. If he stalls, you must determine if it seems profitable to wait any longer. If it doesn't, inform him politely that you intend to seek another placement opportunity.

Once a story has been used, it can be reworked and placed again by approaching the basic material from a different angle.

For example, suppose a business editor has used your story on the importance of the do-it-yourself market to the construction industry. (We are still presuming you are in that business.) You have arranged an interview with one of your financial executives to ensure mention of your company's name in the story.

After the story appears, you might rearrange the material, delete some figures, and change the focus of the piece to emphasize trends in the do-it-yourself movement—what people used to do at home and what they are doing now, how inflation has sent Americans back to their workbenches, and so on. You now have a new story to "pitch" to the do-it-yourself or general-features editor of another newspaper, this time offering a different knowledgeable company executive to be interviewed. A good idea is hard to find. Get all the mileage you can out of it.

Whether you are dealing with hard news or features, it is wise to remember that the most important reality of a newsperson's life is the deadline. Promised material must arrive on time, even if you have to hire a messenger or deliver it personally. Answer a reporter's calls promptly—he or she might be working on a story. When you send out a news release or suggest a feature to a news-

paper person, try to be available at all times. If you are out of the
office and there is no one else who can answer important questions, emphasize to your employees and/or co-workers that this is
top priority and that you are to be contacted if at all humanly
possible. It is by exerting this kind of extra effort that close media
relations are built.

One of the most successful financial-relations people in highly
competitive New York City has given his home telephone number
to every newspaper person with whom he has contact, in the
event they might need him after he has left the office. His dinner
is frequently interrupted and he's been awakened late at night
once or twice, but he enjoys better relations with the press than
any other public relations practitioner in the entire city.

A small but welcome gesture is to show your appreciation
when a story or press release is used. A phone call or short note is
sufficient. Do not thank the reporter. He does not feel that he has
used the material as a favor to you. Simply compliment him on
the accuracy and interest of the story.

THE EDITORIAL INTERVIEW

Within your total program you may be setting up interviews with
many media—magazines, wire services, financial wires, radio, and
television. But since you will be arranging interviews most frequently with the daily press, that is what we will discuss here.

A reporter might request an interview with you or one of your
fellow executives, or you yourself might suggest it. Guidelines
should be established at the time the interview is arranged. There
should be agreement on which areas the person being interviewed
is equipped and willing to discuss. These are the so-called ground
rules. The reporter will occasionally "go fishing," asking questions
outside the established boundaries. You are entitled to remind
him, politely, of the agreement and, if possible, to suggest other
sources for the information he requires.

Let us presume that you, as the public-relations person for
your company, are the one being interviewed. Keep the following
guidelines in mind (or, if the interviewee is another executive,
simply make sure that he or she follows these procedures):

1. Do your homework. Be familiar with the publication for
   which the reporter works. Read some of his by-line stories, if

they are available. Bring along all possible back-up material to substantiate any statements you make.

2. Be friendly and natural even if you have never met the reporter before. You are peers talking for your mutual benefit.

3. Keep the subject of the interview in mind and get to it as quickly as possible. Make your points concisely. If the reporter wants greater detail, he will ask for it.

4. Make sure the approach is always "low key." Do not emphasize your company unless the interview is primarily concerned with it. If you have agreed to talk about the industry, for instance, do so. You are not buying ad space. Company credits will develop naturally.

5. Do not be surprised by what seems to be a naive question. The reporter may be putting himself in the position of the uninformed reader, requesting a basic, simple answer.

6. Be ready to back up any statement with facts.

7. Be aware of the reporter's specific areas of interest.

8. If you don't know an answer, admit it. Offer to get the information if that is possible. If it is not, tell the reporter so. Above all, don't bluff. You are not expected to be the world's greatest expert.

9. If you promise to provide information, deliver it as quickly as possible. (Deadline!)

10. When you have nothing more to say, stop talking. You have no obligation to keep the conversation going. If the reporter wants any further information, he'll ask for it.

11. Never ask the reporter if he is going to use the story. The decision is not his. He must submit it to an editor who will make the final judgment based on the news load that day, similar stories he may have published recently, the material's immediacy, and innumerable other factors. Simply thank the reporter and assure him of your continued cooperation, should it be required.

12. *Never ask to see a story before it is printed.* On many publications, if the reporter were to agree, he would lose his job. Should a newspaper person ever ask you to check a story for accuracy, do just that. Make no comment on the editorial approach. The press is extremely jealous of its independence.

13. And finally, to repeat one of our basic principles, never say anything to a media person "off the record."

These basic precepts apply whenever you are interviewed, no matter which of the media the questioner represents.

PHOTOGRAPHY

The factors that govern photos for the daily press are essentially true for all print media. You should have some knowledge of when and how to use them. A good photograph will often "sell" a marginal story. Many local papers have an overload of written material but a real need for artwork to break up the layout and add interest. But photos cost money and should be used judiciously. It is preferable, of course, to get a commitment from a specific editor in advance. It is possible that he will not have a staff photographer available to cover an event but will indicate, nevertheless, that he could use a photo, if it is good and is supplied to him. Getting the photo, then, will be up to you.

Once having decided to take pictures, you should carefully consider which photographer to hire. Many people working for local papers do freelance work on the side. Retaining such a person has distinct advantages. He or she comes to the assignment with knowledge of the kinds of photos a newspaper uses. If the photographer offers advice on setting up the picture, you should welcome it. If your local paper has a staff photographer who does freelance work, the photo editor will usually be happy to furnish you with this information. The Associated Press and United Press International have commercial photo departments in many cities. These people, too, are experienced news photographers. Their fees will usually be a little higher than local fees because the service itself must make a profit.

If this kind of help is unavailable, find out if any of the commercial photographers in town have news experience. Hire one who lives nearby, since you don't want to pay extensive travel expenses, and supervise him carefully.

Remember that you are not creating a work of art; you are taking a news photo. There are several simple rules to keep in mind:

1. Be aware that the best pictures portray action.
2. Be sure they are in sharp focus or they will not reproduce well.

3. Always take at least two shots of each setup, but three or four are preferable. Once you have hired a photographer, the additional cost will be negligible.
4. If you are going to service more than one publication, come up with a different shot for each one, even if you simply alter the pose, the background, and some of the people involved.
5. Whenever possible, take photos close up.
6. Remember that anything or anybody in the shot should be visible and in focus.
7. If you use objects, try to select light-colored ones. Dark ones will often lose detail or disappear into the background.
8. Avoid deadpan shots and overposing. Try to show some emotion and a casual appearance. Once you have decided what you want, the photographer is in charge of the picture. Let him place and pose the people.
9. Try not to put more than three people in a picture; two, if possible, would be preferable. Group shots are a waste of time and money. They will not be used.
10. Take a picture you would be interested in seeing.

After the photo session is over, have the pictures developed quickly (within an hour or two if possible) as 8-by-10-inch glossy prints. Make sure they are underdeveloped rather than over-developed. Newspaper reproduction will darken them. Make sure that a "cut line" or caption is *pasted* to the back of the picture, which details the event, the people in the picture (from left to right), and all other pertinent data. Do this even if the picture is included with a story or release. In a busy newspaper office, the two items might easily be separated. Never write on the back of a photo.

Most important, remember that a news photo is just that—news. Get it to the paper more quickly than seems humanly possible. This might entail pushing the photographer (who will auto-matically tell you, "it can't be done in that amount of time"), and having someone wait in his studio while the pictures are devel-oped, with the captions, paste pot, and releases in hand, ready to assemble the package and run it over to the paper. The closer to the actual event you can get the photo to the editor, the better the chance of its being used.

Finally, never send a paper a picture that you know is bad.

Sometimes, despite all your efforts, you just do not get usable shots. If you have promised pictures to an editor, call him and tell him the truth, or reshoot if you have the time. The editor will realize that you are knowledgeable and that you would rather lose a placement than provide inadequate material.

THE WIRE SERVICES

Servicing the two wires is very similar to your approach to the daily press. Include them in your general mailings of hard news and consider them a potential market for feature stories. Always work through your local bureau. If the story requires handling at the bureaus' national headquarters (they are both located in New York City), let the local reporter initiate the contact.

When you are deciding whether a feature idea is better for the daily press or for the wire services, a good criterion is broadness of interest. If the story has a "local" slant, it is good for the daily press. If it has national or regional implications, you might want to try for the extensive coverage that the wire services provide.

To a certain extent, you can control this yourself. If, for example, you are suggesting a story on the increasing use of certain products in home building, you might gather national statistics to lead off your wire-service story, and local figures as the anchor for your daily-press pitch. Again, respect exclusivity. Do not try to place one story until the other has appeared or been rejected.

THE BUSINESS NEWS WIRES

Dow-Jones and Reuters should be included in your distribution of hard news. However, if your company has a corporate public-relations department, it is probable that it has already built close relationships with these financial news wires.

If not, you should approach Dow-Jones every six months to propose a wire story on your company. This move is usually based on a "hard news" hook such as quarterly or annual performance figures, expansion plans, stock offerings, and so forth. The Dow-Jones reporter will usually want to interview your chief executive officer or the executive most knowledgeable about corporate development. In most cases a Dow-Jones ticker story will appear the next day in the *Wall Street Journal.* Unless you have news of tremendous import, twice a year should be your maximum expectation for stories from Dow-Jones. At the end of those quarters when you do not approach Dow-Jones, you should suggest a similar story to Reuters, which operates in much the same way.

Remember, if you have a corporate public-relations department, coordinate your effort with them before contacting either of these wires. The wire services should not be deluged with material from different people in the same company.

OTHER NEWS MEDIA

TRADE PAPERS AND MAGAZINES

You are aware of the importance of these publications. Hard news should, usually, be distributed to your entire trade list.

From time to time you will have a news item of interest to one or two segments of your trade list—a product that is important to one or two industries alone, new designs slanted toward a specific market, and so forth. This is why you have set up your trade list to be used either as a whole or in sections.

These publications are prime targets for feature placements. Become familiar with the particular needs of each paper and book. You will quickly discover the kinds of material they use. Among the story ideas that might be appropriate are industry trends and predictions, new products, case histories, inventive uses for old products, interviews with company officers on plans for the future, opinions and positions on general industry problems.

The trade-press reporters should be treated with the same courtesy and consideration that you extend to the daily press. They are equally important to you. The same strict rules of exclusivity apply.

THE ELECTRONIC MEDIA

This is a tough nut, but it can be cracked. Several different approaches are possible. As a matter of course, all hard-news releases should be sent to the news editors on your electronic-media list. The material will seldom be used as sent, but it might create interest in some phase of your operation.

Occasional events may warrant coverage by local radio and television people. These might include the opening of a facility that is significant to the area's economy (your chances of coverage are improved if important people—that is, the mayor, a senator, U.S. representative, governor, federal official—are present), the presentation of a large prize in a contest, the visit of a national celebrity, such as a well-known entertainer or politician, to your plant.

Before contacting radio or television, carefully consider the visual and audio possibilities of the occasion. If you decide they are good, there are certain procedures to follow:

1. Contact the assignment editor of the channel or station, *not* your favorite anchorperson, the news director, or anyone else. The assignment editor determines what will be covered.
2. Send this editor the announcement of the event and all pertinent back-up material well in advance, and follow up with a phone call. You will usually be told that it is too soon to schedule. Also, it might be suggested that you try a phone call the day before the event itself is scheduled to take place. Be sure to make that second call—whether it's been suggested or not. You will probably be given a definite no or be told that your event has been put on the schedule. This does not mean that it will be covered. That will depend on what else is happening that particular day.
3. If possible, schedule the event between 10:00 A.M. and 2:30 P.M. on a weekday. Coverage must be completed by midafternoon for tape to be processed in time for the early evening news show.
4. Make the event visual for television coverage.
5. Make interview subjects available for radio coverage.
6. If you have a definite commitment for television coverage, wait for the cameras as long as possible. They are frequently late. Keep the print newspeople busy with industry talk, refreshments, or discussions of matters that are not part of the actual event.
7. If a statement is being made, make sure it is short and direct. If it is a visual event, stage it quickly and effectively. You are

basically trying to get sixty seconds of television time and, perhaps, twice as much on radio.

8. Remember that no company representative should say anything on mike or camera that the world should not know. The "slip," the "off-the-record" comment, the "aside" which is regretted in retrospect, is usually what the media uses.

Another entry into television and radio is through the local interview and talk shows whose producers you have included on your list. Watch or listen to each show and determine the kinds of guests it uses. If you believe that one of the people in your speakers' bureau (see Chapter 8) would fit into the format of a particular show, send the producer a background kit. This should include pictures, education and work experience, present duties, and subjects that the proposed guest is qualified to discuss. The kit might not result in an immediate appearance, but the producer will keep it on file, and should he be planning a program into which your candidate's expertise would fit, he will know where to call.

Television interview concepts are much like print feature ideas, except a greater possibility of success exists if they have visual interest. Depending upon your activities, of course, some of the program ideas you might suggest are:

How-To Features
This could be a do-it-yourself demonstration using your company's products.

Trend Stories
These may be new ideas involving your unit's products or services, developments related to "hot" items in the news, such as energy, the economy, unemployment, and so on.

Industry Stories
These include the market for your company's particular products or services, how your industry can help combat inflation and recession, government and industry cooperation or conflict, and so forth.

Personality Interviews
If you have an unusual and colorful person in your speakers' file— a fine artist, a third- or fourth-generation employee, someone with

a startling or dramatic hobby—he or she might fit into many television and radio talk shows.

As suggested, keep abreast of the news and attempt to tie into it. If there is a sudden increase or decrease in new housing starts in one month, and you are in that business, you can assume that news directors and talk-show producers will be looking for knowledgeable people to discuss the subject. Get on the phone and offer them such a person if you have one available. You will achieve better results than you might expect. The editor or producer has a lot of air space to fill up day after day. He is always looking for sound, interesting, not overly commercial ideas.

MAGAZINES

You should, as a matter of course, distribute hard-news releases to the news magazines on an FYI ("for your information") basis. The procedure for placing a feature in these magazines is the same as with the daily press. Send a pitch letter outlining the concept, the background material you have, the people available for interviews, and other pertinent information. Follow up with phone calls, respect exclusivity, and function as if you were contacting a newspaper.

However, two additional factors are involved. Your suggestion must have national interest and it must be consistent with the news magazine's format and weekly publication schedule. These magazines cannot compete with the dailies in terms of immediacy, so they must contribute additional depth to any subject with which they deal. For *Time* or *Newsweek*, for example, you cannot rehash material that you have sent to the daily press. You must offer them fresh insight on subjects that have already been reported in a general fashion.

WEEKLIES, SHOPPERS, CLUB PAPERS

Send your hard-news releases to this list. In addition, these papers present excellent placement possibilities for stories that have been turned down by the dailies or for reworked versions of those already used.

These smaller publications present one problem. They are extremely short-staffed. The weeklies will follow up on a story lead if it does not require too large an investment of time. The shoppers and club papers usually require a finished story. This might not be worth the time and effort required on your part. However, if you have a finished story on hand, for whatever reason, think of these publications as a placement market.

A little wooing of the editors of the weeklies will go a long way. They don't get as much of it as their colleagues on the dailies. The fact that you have the name of the correct editor on your media list will please them, as will a follow-up call after sending them a release. You will not want to spend a great deal of time on these papers, but if you are in the neighborhood on other business, a courtesy call on an editor will probably make a media friend.

FEATURE SERVICES

These services are particularly helpful if you have a feature idea that has been turned down by AP and UPI but that you think has real merit. The feature wires go to hundreds of papers throughout the country and can have great impact. If you have such a national-interest feature in mind, consider them as a prime placement possibility.

THE PRESS CONFERENCE

A well-known practitioner of public relations once defined hell as a twenty-four-hour-a-day press conference. That is a fairly accurate description.

So many things can, and often do, go wrong at press conferences that they should, as a general rule, be avoided. Unless the subject matter is of intense, immediate interest and importance, it is all but impossible to get significant media representation. Nervous public-relations people frequently fill these meetings with "freeloaders" and peripheral newspeople, which does the sponsoring organization little good.

Should the attendance level be successful, the press conference still must be controlled so that it doesn't become a free-for-all at which statements are made without advance consideration, quite possibly to be regretted later on.

You will seldom have occasion to hold a press conference. Exceptions might be an emergency (see Chapter 6 for a discussion of public relations in an emergency) or some development of almost staggering national or regional import.

Should you have the need for such a project, check with your corporate public-relations department, if your company has one. If not, coordinate it with the office of the chief executive officer.

The above sections are designed to aid you in gaining the knowledge of various media that are important to your unit's public-relations program. However, it is impossible to define completely the growing, ever-changing communications scene. Public-relations reference volumes and publications will help keep you up to date (a list of these is included in the bibliography).

3

HOW TO WRITE A
NEWS RELEASE

Before we break down the mechanics of news-release writing, it would be a good idea to outline some of the general principles governing the procedure.

WHAT IS A NEWS STORY?

A news story answers some basic questions. Foremost is "What happened?" or "What is going to happen?" In order to understand the event, however, it is also necessary to answer:

To whom did it happen?   Where did it happen?
How did it happen?   Why did it happen?
When did it happen?

Of course, this has been summed up by editors since time immemorial as the "what, who, how, when, where, and why." Every news release you send out must answer these questions or it should not go out at all.

In order for the event to be newsworthy, it must contain one or more of these elements:

timeliness	romance
human interest	meaningful predictions
public interest	money
well-known people	exclusivity
conflict	sex
mystery	novelty
tragedy	humor

Your releases will usually be based on timeliness, public interest, conflict, human interest, or information or speculation about the future, but look for all these elements.

As we have emphasized, there is no guarantee that your release will be used, but if you prepare it properly you will increase its chances of becoming a story.

Your release should have a general objective but be written for a specific audience. It should be interesting and timely and, once again, it must answer the editor's questions: what, who, how, when, where, and why.

Your news release should resemble a pyramid in construction. The first paragraph should tell the essential story very briefly, and the succeeding paragraphs should amplify and elaborate, each giving greater detail and background. It is your job to assist the editor to do his or her job. If your story is too long for the space available, he or she will cut from the bottom of the release. If the editor can't do that, your story is likely to be discarded and another story of approximate news value will be used instead. Your story must be complete even if the last few paragraphs are cut.

In addition, the reader will tend to glance at the first paragraph and not read the entire story. You want to give him or her the necessary information early on.

MECHANICS OF PRESS RELEASES

A release to any news medium should be typed, double-spaced on 8½-by-11-inch white paper with wide margins on both sides (you are supplying plenty of room for the editor to use his or her blue pencil). Type on only one side of the page. Try to limit all releases to one page, but if that is not possible, then be sure to number each page, and at the bottom of each page, except the last, type: "(more)." A sentence or paragraph should never be split between two pages. The old news tradition of using the symbol -30- to end a story is out of fashion. Now, either the date or three asterisks (° ° °) is usual.

A headline should indicate the contents of the release. Although this headline will seldom, if ever, be used by the paper, it can influence acceptance of the item. For instance, COMPANY EX-ECUTIVE DELIVERS SPEECH is a dull headline. The same release might be entitled, CHAIRMAN SUGGESTS ALTERNATIVE ENERGY

SOURCES (or whatever he is discussing). The second headline obviously has more news interest.

Below you will find a typical news release. The numbers refer to the corresponding notes that follow the release and explain its various elements. If you have little experience in this area, use the text of the release and the covering notes to give yourself some foundation.

ABC Division   1.
Company X
345 Smith Street
Pawling, New York 12345

CONTACT: James Stewart, Assistant to the Manager   2.
            Telephone: (914) 555-5666

FOR IMMEDIATE RELEASE   3.

COMPANY X APPOINTS DIVISION MANAGER   4.

PAWLING, N.Y. -- Robert E. Less has been appointed   5.
manager of the ABC Division of Company X, the nation's
largest producer of left-handed wrenches, John Johnson,
Company X president, announced today.

"The appointment of Bob Less is an example of the   6.
company's policy of building management strength from
within," Mr. Johnson said. "We are confident that he
will continue to make an important contribution to our
success."

Mr. Less, who will serve on the corporate executive   7.
committee in his new position, was previously assistant
to the manager of the ABC Division and has been with
the company in an executive capacity for fourteen years.

(more)   8.

ABC, the company's largest division, manufactures the   9.
wrenches that are the company's most popular product.

Mr. Less will be executive as well as operational chief of the division.

Mr. Less was president of the Less Wrench Company before joining Company X. He is a graduate of MIT and holds a degree in business administration from the Harvard Business School. He lives with his wife, Martha, and three children in Peekskill, New York.　10.

Mr. Less replaces Alfred Ingliss as division manager. Mr. Ingliss has resigned in order to concentrate on private business matters.　11.

5/15/80　　　　　　　　12.

NOTES ON RELEASE

1. If you send the release out on your letterhead, be sure to note that it is a news release and use the letterhead only for the first page.
2. Even if you use a letterhead, the name and phone number of the correct contact must also be typed in. This is the person ready and able to answer questions. He or she must be available to take calls.
3. Try to label all stories FOR IMMEDIATE RELEASE. It presents fewer problems to the editor. If absolutely necessary, however, you may say: FOR RELEASE ON OR AFTER AUGUST 12, 1982, or FOR RELEASE AUGUST 25, 1982, AFTER 9 A.M.
4. This is a pedestrian but informative headline. A more interesting alternative might be, COMPANY BUILDS MANAGEMENT FROM WITHIN.
5. The city of origin should appear at the beginning of the news release. This first paragraph tells your story. If the editor chooses to use it alone, you will have accomplished your objective.
6. This is important because it states company philosophy and provides the chief executive with exposure, so you put it near the top in the hope that it will be used.
7. Simply expands the basic story.
8. Make sure that "(more)" is on every page but the last.
9. (Same as 7.)

10. This is a paragraph you do not expect the large dailies to use. You put it in for the papers in Peekskill and the alumni publications of MIT and Harvard.
11. This is a paragraph that you would like to lose. Mr. Ingliss retired with some resentment but he agreed to the explanation used in the release. You include it in an attempt to satisfy the editor's questions before he asks them.
12. The date should appear at some place in every release.

4

HOW TO WRITE A
PITCH LETTER

The pitch letter is one of your primary tools of communication with the media. You will use it to place feature stories, set up interviews, obtain coverage for press conferences and special events, and for a number of other purposes.

Since the uses for a pitch letter are so varied, the kinds of tight rules that apply to the writing of a news release do not apply to the composition of a pitch letter. The pitch letter permits a much greater use of your imagination and initiative.

THE MECHANICS

Write your pitch letter exactly as you would any business letter, using your regular stationery. If your title appears on the letterhead, do not repeat it under your signature.

Leave plenty of white space, write several short paragraphs rather than a few long ones, and, in general, make the letter easy to read.

Be sure that your name and phone number appear prominently. If there are specific hours when you can be reached, include that information in the letter.

Unless the story you are pitching is as world-shaking as a war or a natural disaster, or as complicated as Einstein's theory of relativity, keep your letter down to a page or a page and a half. Newspeople are deluged with releases and resent unnecessary padding.

THE CONTENT OF THE LETTER

Although pitch-letter form is freer than that of a news release, the pitch letter must answer the same questions: what, who, how, when, where, and why. However, it does not impose the same limitations. You do not have to tell your story in the first paragraph. You can use the opening lines to grab the reader's attention, to sell the entire concept of the story.

Your letter must accomplish several objectives. It must:

1. present the concept of the story;
2. summarize the facts supporting the story;
3. list the material you have available: statistics, graphics, photos, and so forth;
4. offer an interview on your story subject with an expert, if there is one available;
5. suggest a follow-up for the letter.

Since this tool has so many applications, we will not attempt to write a "typical" letter. Instead, we will offer several letters and opening paragraphs that actually were used in specific situations. It may be that none of them will be relevant to your particular company, but they will serve to broaden your awareness of the versatility and effectiveness of the technique.

EXAMPLE 1.

In order to make it timely, try to tie your letter into a newsworthy event or trend. The following example was used several years ago by a computer-leasing company and achieved excellent results:

Mr. John Smith
The Iowa Dispatch
123 Main Street
Crowley, Iowa 13579

Dear Mr. Smith: *(or first name, if you are on that basis)*
    As you know, today XYZ announced a radical change in pricing policies. The cost of equipment has been slashed and

rental prices have been increased. The obvious purpose of this move is to encourage cash sales and discourage rentals. The reason is that XYZ must improve its cash position.

One of the immediate effects of this development is that it provides an absolute bonanza for computer-leasing companies. These companies buy equipment from XYZ (which makes XYZ very happy) and lease it for 15 percent less than XYZ does (which makes the customers equally happy).

The new XYZ pricing policy means that leasing companies will be able to pass on an additional 4- to 6-percent savings to their customers.

Grandex Computer Leasing Company is one of the largest in the field. I am enclosing their annual report and other relevant information. Company and industry statistics on growth, trends, and future prospects are available for use in a story on this mushrooming sector of a space-age industry.

Mr. Gerald Gerald, president of Grandex, is a computer engineer and a pioneer in computer rental. He has a degree in business administration from the Harvard Business School. He will be in this city from July 10 through July 17. I would be happy to arrange an interview at your convenience. I'm sure you will find Mr. Gerald informative and imaginative.

I will call you in a few days to discuss this story possibility.

Sincerely,

John Doe

JD/gg
Enclosures

You will notice that this letter accomplishes the objectives we outlined: it presents the concept of the story; it summarizes some of the facts supporting the story; it lists additional available material; it offers an expert to be interviewed; and it suggests a follow-up phone call.

In addition, the letter takes advantage of a recent development of which the editor should be aware. This is a great strength, and you should be alert to similar possibilities. For example, if housing starts fall off dramatically for a month or a quarter and your target publication prints that news, you might suggest a story on the way in which the repair and remodeling industry is taking up the slack. Your lead might be:

Mr. John Smith
The Iowa Dispatch
123 Main Street
Crowley, Iowa 13579

Dear Mr. Smith:

The new cry of the American homeowner seems to be, "if you can't move, improve!"

As you know, last month's new housing starts were off _____ percent from the same month last year. This is not good news for anybody, particularly for construction and building-products companies. However, there is a bright side.

Consumer expenditures for remodeling and improving homes increased a whopping _____ percent over the previous year in the same month that housing starts fell off.

You would then proceed to develop the story; present additional facts; suggest available material; offer one of your officers or yourself for an interview; and tell the editor how you intend to follow up.

EXAMPLE 2

An important development within your unit might serve as the "hook" for a story. If you are sending your letter to a local paper, the unit activity might be enough. If you are approaching a regional, national, or trade publication, you might have to expand the specific event to illustrate a general trend.

When the ABC Division of Company X expanded its production facilities for left-handed wrenches, our imaginary executive sent out the following letter:

Dear Mr. Smith:

In July of this year the ABC Division of Company X will open a new modern facility for the production of left-handed wrenches at Storeyville, Georgia. In addition, the division will expand and modernize existing plants in Boston, New York State, and Oregon.

These expansion moves will make Company X the largest producer of left-handed wrenches in the country.

Important as these developments are to our company and to the industry, they are even more significant as an indication of an emerging national trend.

Industry is no longer ignoring left-handed people. Until now, "southpaws" had to make do with tools, equipment, and artifacts designed for the right-handed majority. American business, ever-open to the lure of new markets, is changing that situation.

We have researched this trend. We have available for you a long list of products from back scratchers to sewing machines, from complicated tools to simple household materials, which are being made specifically for left-handed people.

Irving Irving, vice-president for marketing of Company X, is one of the few specialists in this new area of marketing concentration. He will be in our city from June 5 through June 12. I would be happy to arrange a meeting to discuss the possibilities of this story.

For your information, I am enclosing the annual report and other background information on Company X and a bio of Mr. Irving.

I hope you agree that the "left-handed wrench" can introduce your readers to an interesting and unusual aspect of American business. I will call in a few days to discuss it with you.

Sincerely,

Obviously, you are not making left-handed wrenches. And not every development of your unit will lend itself to such an interesting story idea.

However, whenever there is significant unit activity—the opening of a new facility, the expansion of an existing plant, the introduction of a product line—you should initiate a three-phase program:

1. Send out a news release to all interested media.
2. Consider the possibilities of a pitch letter to local media, based simply on the significance of the development to your company and to the community.
3. Carefully analyze the event as to its broader significance. Does

it indicate a trend? Is it unusual or interesting enough to justify a feature story? Does it relate to current economic or industry news? In short, how can you use this development to get a story in a regional, national, or trade publication?

Of course, you will not be successful in obtaining all three kinds of coverage every time. But it is always worth trying. Unlike an advertisement, a pitch letter costs you only your time and postage. And even if the reporter or editor turns you down, you will have made a new press contact or reinforced one you have already established.

EXAMPLE 3

Perhaps "example" is a misnomer for what follows. The heading might more properly read, "Find the Hook." Every feature story must provide a reason for being used. Sometimes the reason is obvious—John Jones is appointed secretary of commerce; IBM declares bankruptcy; General Motors acquires Ford; and so on. There is no way that a newspaper cannot use a story like that.

However, you will usually be dealing with less earthshaking stories. They will be used or not, depending upon the news judgment of the editor. That judgment can be influenced considerably in your favor if you supply an interesting angle, an unusual approach—a "hook" upon which to hang your material.

There is no way to outline specifically how such an approach can be developed. That will depend upon your imagination and the "nose for news" we discussed earlier.

It helps to have a thorough knowledge of the target publication. Through careful reading and analysis of the stories used therein you will discover ways of shaping your own material to meet the specific requirements of that publication.

In addition, give your imagination full rein as you write. Do not be afraid to be a little "far out," to stretch the bounds of relevance. Your own good taste and business background will prevent you from going too far. Remember, the worst that can happen is that the story will be rejected. And you will learn something from every rejection.

Following are the openings of actual pitch letters that were

successful. The names of the companies and people involved have
been changed, but not the letters themselves. They illustrate how
far from the actual material the hook might be:

Dear John:

Nobody knows what would have happened to the history
of the world if Nero had put down his fiddle and turned his
attention to matters of more importance.

However, we know a man who put away his saxophone
and made millions of dollars for himself. The man is Jim Doe
and he found a pot of gold at both ends of the rainbow—with
two firms making beauty preparations for the professional
beautician. One of the companies is now a giant in the retail
cosmetics field.

Doe started as a successful saxophone player with the
name bands of the thirties. Tired of the traveling and the
"working nights," he took a job as a salesman in the New York
area with Joseph Laboratories, manufacturers and distributors
of supplies and equipment for beauty salons.

The letter proceeded to outline Doe's road to success. Background on the two important companies that he now heads was
enclosed and his availability for an interview was mentioned. The
story was accepted, written, and published by one of the most
prestigious business publications in the country. The editor used
the "saxophone player turned businessman" hook as his lead.

Examine your own background and also interview your fellow
executives as if you were a reporter. You might be surprised to
find a number of interesting angles that you can use to introduce a
story on your unit or its activities.

We offer another example:

Dear Ms. Jones:

Manuel is a man of many worlds. He is of Mexican, Greek,
and Turkish heritage but he is the prototype of the American
business executive. Moreover, his creative efforts provide a
seemingly impossible synthesis of Mexico, Spain, and the
United States.

His full name is Manuel Manuel, and he owns the Fiesta

Shop in Mexico City and the House of Manuel in New York. He may well be the presiding genius of the surge of interest in Mexican and Spanish furniture in this country.

The letter went on to expound Manuel's history and philosophy. Pertinent material was enclosed and an interview was offered. A story in a major metropolitan daily resulted.

This is another example of using an individual to sell a company story. In order for you to do this you must overcome a natural reticence on the part of many business people. You and your colleagues should understand that in presenting yourselves for interviews and as the basis for stories, you are not seeking personal publicity or self-glorification. You are making an important contribution to your company's communications program.

Dear Tanya:

Though diamonds may be a girl's best friend, the ladies seem to prefer pearls. Or, at least, are able to afford pearls, since they are America's most-sold precious jewelry.

The oyster's creations were treasured in China as early as 300 B.C. They are mentioned in the ancient Talmud, the sacred book of Judaism. It says that the clothes Jehovah made for Adam and Eve were "as beautiful as pearls."

The Arab who enters heaven, according to the Koran, lives in a "tent of pearls." And, of course, the New Testament speaks of the "pearly gates" of the new Jerusalem.

The letter went on to relate a number of interesting facts about pearls and then told the history of cultured pearls and of the writer's company, which was the largest importer of cultured pearls in America. It included background on that company and offered the vice-president, a scholar on the history of pearls, as an interviewee.

The result was a feature in a major Sunday supplement which quoted the executive at length and gave excellent coverage of the company itself.

If your unit deals with a product or products, be assured that there is probably an interesting history behind them which can be used to get an editor's attention. Investigate this history, compile a list of unusual facts, and then send out your pitch letters. If one

editor turns you down, there may well be another who is waiting
for just such a story.

The examples are endless, limited only by your imagination. A
good hook can be something very simple—a startling statistic, for
example:

American industry is being buried under a mass of paper.

Business in this country used enough paper in 1979 to stretch
to the moon and back five times, with enough left over to
paper the entire earth.

This was a lead for a pitch for a business-form printing company. There are many such amazing facts to uncover relating to
almost any product.

Here is something on an industry trend:

The United States Armed Services are considering renting
their uniforms. This is consistent with the decision in the last
ten years of most uniform users in private industry to rent
rather than buy.

This story on a uniform-rental company was placed.

In conclusion, in a pitch letter anything that makes sense and
excites interest is acceptable. Remember what the letter must
accomplish. It must present the story concept; include supporting
facts; list available background materials; offer an interview if
possible; and establish a follow-up procedure.

Be imaginative, be creative, but, above all, be persistent. Keep
sending out those letters. If they are rejected by one editor, try
another. If one idea seems not to work, then by all means, try
another.

5

THE ELEMENTS OF A PUBLIC-RELATIONS PROGRAM: THE COMMUNITY

We have noted the importance, to any company, of the communities in which it operates and the public-relations program that affects those communities. This chapter examines in detail various techniques for developing positive and useful community/company relationships.

DEFINING YOUR "AFFECT COMMUNITY"

At this point in your public-relations program you need to determine the confines and components of the community, or communities, in which you do business.

The community includes all people and organizations affected by, or who can affect, your company because of its geographic location. Your community may include employees, shareholders, customers, suppliers, and others with whom you have some direct relationship. But it includes also a great many more people with whom you have no direct involvement.

If you are a giant corporation, your community includes all the people in your plant cities and, to a lesser degree, most of the people in the United States. If you are multinational, your community will be worldwide.

Your particular community is probably more limited. It cannot, however, be determined by simple physical boundaries. It is more than a neighborhood, city, region, or state. It extends just as far as the effects of your actions reach.

For example, a company that pollutes the streams and waterways may affect people who live in the neighboring state or the one beyond that. Those people become part of the company's "affect community."

Make sure you are aware of your community's specific problems, its interests, its economic situation, its political position, and its special emotional attitudes.

Community complaints are seldom directed to the company that is considered guilty. One person will, generally, complain to another, and the dissatisfaction will grow and snowball while the company is still unaware of it. To prevent this from happening, you must understand your community and its needs and concerns, and address those concerns before the relationship is jeopardized.

Start by listing organizations and individuals with whom you wish to maintain a dialogue. In preparing such lists, include:

- Opinion leaders
- Groups and individuals who possess economic power
- Significant politicians and political organizations
- Environmental groups
- Churches, synagogues, and other religious bodies
- Civic and fraternal organizations
- Cultural institutions
- Trade, labor, and business organizations
- All other groups and people who appear to have influence in molding community attitudes

This will be your work list for community action.

TOTAL COMMUNITY RELATIONS

There are some general guidelines for good community relations. There must be a corporate sensitivity to issues that concern the community such as noise levels, pollution control, and the appearance of an installation and its environs.

The company should make an effort to keep local and regional government agencies apprised of the company's activities and sympathetic to its objectives.

Community participation in events such as plant openings and tours can create a feeling of friendship and involvement. Most important, information regarding all positive aspects of the company's performance must be communicated continuously to the targeted public—in this case, the people who live in the area. The company is of real significance to the economic well-being of the towns, cities, localities, and states in which it operates. It employs people, pays taxes, represents buying power, and is, in many ways, a key element in maintaining the desired life-style. These contributions must be made clear to the citizens on a consistent basis in a forceful and intelligent manner.

In no facet of your program is it truer that public relations is good performance, publicly appreciated. We must, therefore, discuss two phases of· this segment of the work—performance, and the reporting of that performance, in order to win the desired appreciation.

These are some of the basic elements of good community-relations performance:

1. A regard for the appearance of your unit. It should be clean, attractive, and fit into the surrounding area in a way that is as aesthetically pleasing as possible.
2. An awareness of pollutants that your unit might be releasing into the air or water supply and a concentrated effort to eliminate such emissions.
3. A similar awareness of noise and odor problems and a vigorous attempt to control them.
4. A concentrated effort to adjust to the community's traffic patterns without disrupting them.
5. An involvement in all reasonable projects to protect and conserve the natural resources and ambiance of the area.
6. A quick, courteous, and concerned handling of all complaints from the community. No matter how unfair they may appear, regardless of your inability to act in certain circumstances, every complaint should be addressed individually and answered thoroughly and sincerely.
7. Maintenance of working conditions within your unit on a level that will assure the approval of the entire community.
8. Participation in community-service activities (discussed later in this chapter).
9. An effort to purchase materials and supplies on a local level. This should be discussed with company headquarters.

All these elements will achieve only minimal results unless you have made your community aware of them. This communication can take several forms.

COMMUNITY INVOLVEMENT

Invite your unit's neighbors to plant openings; organize tours of the various facilities for church, school, and other groups; initiate periodic "open houses" where community members and your unit's executives can exchange ideas on mutual problems (and, ideally, satisfactions); investigate the possibility of hosting parties on occasions of particular significance to the area, such as the anniversary of a city's founding.

MEDIA ACTIVITIES

As we have seen, an effective placement program in the local media will be of great significance in communicating with your community. In all material emanating from your unit, the feelings, sensitivities, opinions, and concerns of your community should be considered.

DIRECT COMMUNICATION

By using the list of leaders and organizations that you have compiled, you will establish direct communication with your community. You should send to all the people on this list copies of all pertinent news releases, corporate financial messages, invitations, announcements, and specifically designed material when the need arises. Every effort should be made to establish dialogue between your unit and these organizations and individuals. You should also solicit replies to your communications. Only in this way will you be made aware of problems early enough to solve them with minimum disruption of relationships.

Another important element should be mentioned in this section. Since local, regional, and federal government agencies in your area are important members of your "affect community," you must be concerned with them as well. This is obviously a sensitive area. Except under unusual circumstances, your communications with government personnel should be confined to the regular mailing of company-approved material to the list of such people and agencies that you have already compiled. If special information is requested or particular problems surface, corporate headquarters should be consulted first. Policy decisions might be involved, and those are made by the offices of the chairman and the president.

OPEN HOUSES, DEDICATIONS, AND TOURS

Open houses can have a variety of specific purposes: to display a new installation; to observe some special occasion, such as an anniversary or a significant production or safety achievement; to participate in some local civic celebration; or at the official dedication of new facilities or equipment. An open house may be scheduled purely for the benefits to be derived. The results—and the problems—are the same.

The facility should be given every possible preparation to make it attractive, clean, and convenient for the guests. Displays should be arranged and signs erected to designate tour routes. Special guides should be selected and instructed. Refreshments may be served and literature and/or souvenirs distributed. Invitations may be extended to the public-at-large, to special groups, or to both. Films or talks may be scheduled.

A dedication ceremony can serve as an important means of gaining community recognition and of involving local business and civic leaders in your communications program. It is an important platform for favorable publicity as well.

For any dedication ceremony, invitations should come from your company's top official (or the executive of the particular installation).

Tours of company facilities are handled in much the same manner as open houses or dedications, but less preparation is required and fewer people are involved. Tours can be scheduled on a regular basis, one or two guides are the only unit personnel required. Regular tour days may be established or requests from groups may be accepted with a few days' notice.

Your company's management might encourage tours by civic clubs, professional societies, women's or men's groups, youth or senior citizen groups, high-school science or business classes, teachers, clergymen, government officials (with prior clearance from the corporate headquarters), suppliers, dealers, and others. Printed material should be distributed to tour groups and, if it is feasible, simple refreshments may be served. If at all possible, a company executive should take a few minutes to welcome each tour group.

Children under twelve should not be admitted to production facilities, and safety precautions should be taken whatever the event.

When a general invitation is to be made for open houses and dedications, it should be done through the local newspapers and radio and television stations. In addition, letters should be sent to the heads of local organizations, to school officials, the press, and other opinion molders.

In the case of a tour, or if only a particular, special group is being invited to a dedication or open house, the invitation should of course be extended by letter.

The check list on the following pages will be of help in planning open houses and dedications. Certain items will be applicable to tour planning and preparation.

A CHECK LIST

Objectives
- Facilitate good community relations
- Facilitate good employee relations
- Illustrate company or unit policies and benefits
- Demonstrate how products are made
- Dramatize free enterprise in action
- Convey company, unit, and industry message
- Attract prospective employees
- Create new customers
- Support the company's securities
- Other_____

Who Is in Charge?
- Consult with executive in charge of installation
- Appoint committee, if needed
- Name coordinator, if needed
- Advise supervisors and obtain their support
- Choose staff, hosts, guides, lecturer
- Notify employees
- Designate press officer

Guest List—Whom to Invite
- Employees and families
- Customers and prospective customers
- Civic leaders, opinion molders
- Shareholders, financial community members (with prior corporate approval)
- Educators
- Suppliers
- Clergy
- Dealers, jobbers, distributors
- Retired employees
- Youth, men's, women's, and senior-citizen groups
- Business and science classes
- Professional societies
- Officials of other companies
- Special guests suggested by executives

Setting the Time and Date
- Tie in with company or unit anniversary or special event
- Check with other local events to avoid conflicts
- Choose least busy day of week
- Consider a school holiday so entire family might attend
- Set alternate date in case of bad weather
- Set plan for announcing change, if necessary

The Budget
- Estimate attendance
- Check cost of refreshments, catering services, supplies, decorations, special safety precautions, rented films, hired speaker
- Check cost of printing, displays, signs
- Check cost of identification badges
- Check cost of souvenirs, prizes
- Figure mailing expense, postage, press releases
- Figure cost of transportation, if required

Facilities
- Select and mark adequate parking space; assign attendant(s)
- Locate large convenient reception area
- Establish simple registration procedure; assign staff
- Designate ample checkroom space, if required; assign attendant(s)
- Prepare facilities to be seen:
    1. All facilities must be clean and neat
    2. Machinery must be clean, in good working order
    3. Tour route must be absolutely safe

4. Information signs and arrows must be installed
   - Arrange for adequate space to serve refreshments
   - Install or test public-address system for music and announcements
   - Put up suitable displays
   - Make sure rest rooms are convenient, clean, and clearly marked
   - Provide box for drawing if prize is to be given
   - Brief guides and have practice run
   - Give guides uniform explanation of machines and processes
   - Instruct guides to be precise and nontechnical

Format for Tour
   - Arrange for short welcome speech by official
   - Show film, if available
   - Limit size of groups for better handling
   - Route tours to save time and steps, to avoid unattractive areas, to ensure safety and smooth, rapid movement of guests
   - Demonstrate how quality is built into products
   - Illustrate how standards are maintained
   - Demonstrate safety and health precautions
   - Tour modern offices as well as plant
   - Include recreation areas, lounge, library, cafeteria facilities
   - Schedule question-and-answer period at end of tour
   - Note problems for consideration in preparation for subsequent tour or open house

Refreshments
   - Select only quick-service items
   - Contract for cafeteria or catering service to handle refreshments
   - Check on adequate paper containers and disposable utensils
   - Arrange for necessary waste containers

Printed Material
   - Invitations
   - Return postcards, if required
   - Mimeographed instruction for guides
   - Company and industry literature
   - Programs, if required
   - Identification cards or badges
   - Maps of building layout and tour route, if required
   - Registration forms or book
   - Cards for drawing, if prize is given

Displays
   - Prepare displays on scope

of company's activities and operations, photos of other facilities, importance to community

- Prepare displays explaining working of equipment
- Prepare displays of company products
- Prepare displays conveying company and industry messages

Souvenirs and Prizes

- Select inexpensive souvenir bearing company logo and name, if occasion warrants
- If company produces consumer products, consider a door prize made up of a selection of products

Publicity

- Invite press, television, and radio in advance and follow up on invitations the day of the event
- Distribute news releases in advance of the event
- Place advertising as an invitation in advance of event, if needed
- Prepare material for reporters who attend
- Arrange for company

executives to be available for interviews at reporter's request

- Make sure that company press officer maintains contact with all reporters throughout the event
- Arrange for your photographer to cover the event
- Distribute follow-up news release and photos to local and area media while event is in progress
- Use the event as a springboard to place feature stories and interviews

Follow-Up

- Encourage comments and suggestions from visitors
- Give recognition to employees who worked on project
- Hold critique to analyze and improve procedures
- Maintain file of correspondence, news releases, reports, work sheets, media coverage, for future use
- Consider sending photographs and/or follow-up letter to key people who attended

SPECIAL EVENTS

AN IDEA LIST

Open Houses
- Anniversary of company's founding or acquisition
- Anniversary of the opening of a facility
- Other company anniversaries
- Industry events
- Completion of new facilities or offices
- Purchase of facilities or entrance into new community
- Significant achievements, such as production or safety records
- Announcement of new process or product
- Community events, such as salutes to industry, historical commemorations, Business-Education Day, Junior Chamber of Commerce Day

Dedications, Celebrations, and Similar Ceremonies
- Dedication of new facilities
- Dedication of new equipment, office buildings
- Dedication of new parks, employee recreation areas
- Dedication of historical markers or commemorative plaques on company property
- Ground breakings, laying of cornerstones
- First batch of a new product produced

Tours
- In connection with other events, such as students during Public School Week, professional societies during the week honoring their profession
- Press tours in connection with any newsworthy announcement
- An annual tour by retired employees
- Tours by college classes for recruitment or customer-development program
- Regular tour days: publicize the day and time when guides will be available to conduct tours for anyone who appears

Other Events
- Banquets, luncheons, dinners on special occasions to which opinion molders are invited
- Annual reunion of retired employees
- Presentation of scholarships, safety awards
- Executive or employee retirement ceremony

COMMUNITY SERVICE

The surrounding communities will be more friendly and cooperative if the company becomes involved in service activities that benefit the residents.

This entails executives and employees becoming active in charitable, fraternal, and other organizations, as individuals and, in certain instances, as representatives of the company.

It may involve providing financial assistance and, in some cases, materials and equipment to aid these organizations in their tasks.

It may be valuable for company executives to investigate the possibilities of its facilities being used for shelter, first-aid, and other purposes in the event of emergencies or disasters. If this is feasible, contingency plans should be drawn up in cooperation with the responsible civilian and government authorities.

Once again, it is nonproductive for the company to hide its light under the proverbial bushel. In order for its contributions to do the most good—for the community in which it functions and as a positive reflection on the company itself—its activities must be properly publicized.

Setting aside for the moment the civic responsibilities attendant on your role as a corporate employee, you will, presumably, as a private individual, want to make a contribution to your town, city, state, and country. By doing so, without consideration of personal gain, you will automatically help to accomplish one or more of the important objectives of your company's public-relations program.

Become active in those organizations that interest and move you, groups whose objectives you strongly support. There are general charities such as the United Fund, Catholic Charities, the Federation of Jewish Philanthropies; those directed to a single problem or group of problems such as cancer or heart disease; miscellaneous groups such as Big Brothers or Big Sisters, Boy Scouts or Girl Scouts; organizations such as the Masons, Knights of Columbus; civic and businessmen's groups such as the Rotary, Chamber of Commerce; local churches and synagogues; colleges and other educational institutions—all these and many more deserve your support.

PUBLIC AFFAIRS

The extent to which any company becomes involved in the issues
and problems that confront its industry and the nation is a decision to be made at top-management echelons. No matter what
policy is established, carrying it out becomes an important element of the public-relations program employing a broad range of
tools and techniques.

6

PUBLIC RELATIONS IN AN EMERGENCY

It is most difficult to maintain good public and press relations when an accident or emergency occurs. In such situations there are persistent, seemingly unrelenting inquiries from the press, the community, business associates, government agencies, friends and relatives of employees, and other interested people. Fatigue and tension can cause short tempers and lapses in efficiency. Unless great care is taken, months of good public-relations work can be undone in a single day.

A delicate balance must be achieved between refusing to answer questions at all and giving hasty and ill-conceived responses. On the one hand, the company can be accused of withholding vital information. On the other, partial or unclear answers can result in unfavorable stories and false rumors.

However, providing good emergency services for the media can earn friends for the company regardless of the nature and scope of the problem.

Presumably the company has an excellent safety record. Thorough precautions have been taken to eliminate accidents. The company does not anticipate any serious incidents, but it must have a plan for dealing with such contingencies or it may well be considered incompetent and poorly managed, should an emergency arise.

The following emergency operations and communications policy is adaptable for several corporate setups, with logical modifications determined by the nature of the specific company:

An authorized spokesperson, usually the unit's senior executive, should be designated in advance to represent management on the scene and to be responsible for the implementation of this program.

If there is a person other than the senior executive who is in

charge of the unit's public-relations program, he or she
should automatically assume the responsibilities of press
officer. If not, a press officer for emergencies should be
designated in advance by the senior executive.

The senior executive should assure that the chief executive
officer is immediately informed of the nature of the
emergency and is kept constantly up to date on all
developments for the duration of the problem.

Factual information on all personnel injuries should be given
to the employees' families as soon as the senior executive
has confirmed the facts. If at all possible, this information
should not be given to the media until after the families
have been notified.

The press officer should provide the media with information as
soon as facts can be verified, and within the parameters of
company policy.

No company employee should speculate on anything that has
not been positively and officially verified, such as the cause
of an accident. The company should take the initiative in
informing the press and local government authorities if they
are not already aware of the situation.

Reporters and photographers should be permitted access to
company property when, and only when, their safety can be
absolutely guaranteed. If there is any question regarding the
safety of the site, the media should be provided with a
steady stream of current information and should be advised
that they will be permitted to visit the scene when the
situation has been stabilized.

No company employee should release any damage estimates
or construction costs until they are officially assessed and
issued by the senior executive.

The press officer, and all company personnel, should
emphasize to the media the company's safety record and
the continuing precautions taken to avoid accidents.

The press officer should utilize all means of communication to
provide factual information to offset rumors or
misstatements; the company should, as quickly as possible,
inform all interested publics, including employees' families,
shareholders, the financial community, suppliers, customers,

members of the "affect community," and, of course, all media.

WHAT CONSTITUTES AN EMERGENCY?

A public-relations emergency is a situation or event that may be interpreted in a manner which could or would be harmful to the company, and that is subject to coverage by the news media in a way that is not in the interests of the company. Such emergencies include, but are not limited to:

- A plant accident involving serious injuries or fatalities
- Any event that requires the assistance of such outside agencies as police, fire, or medical
- An explosion or fire
- Death of a company executive from causes that appear to be related to his or her official duties
- A riot or civil disorder on or near company property
- A so-called act of God—a natural disaster such as an earthquake or flood

In short, any incident or situation that focuses unusual media and public attention on the company must be considered a public-relations emergency.

EMERGENCY PROCEDURES

Immediately upon becoming aware of the emergency, the senior executive (who is the executive in charge), should alert the designated press officer. (Each of these people should appoint substitutes to back them up in case they are unavailable when an emergency occurs.)

The senior executive should confirm that the police, fire department, and so on, have been properly alerted and then should inform the company chief executive officer.

The press officer should contact the corporate public-relations office, if such a department exists. If the situation warrants, a member of that department should proceed immediately to the location to assist in press relations and to provide counsel when required.

PRESS HEADQUARTERS

Each unit should designate two locations—a primary and an alternate—to serve as central media information points in case of a serious emergency. Each location should be equipped with a number of telephones and adequate office equipment. These may, of course, be facilities that are normally used for regular business purposes.

If the emergency is centered in or near the primary press location, then the alternate area should be utilized. Employees should be informed of these plans in advance so that they will be able to direct reporters.

At least two secretaries should be assigned to the press officer to take calls from media people, whether or not a press headquarters has been established. If the press officer is unavailable to take calls, all of them should be listed, and he or she should return them as promptly as possible.

PRESS RELATIONS

Upon notification of the emergency the press officer should assess available information and determine if a press headquarters is required and, if so, at which of the predesignated locations it should be established. The seriousness of the situation influences the need for such a facility, which can help keep media people out of the way of rescue personnel and facilitate the accurate, prompt delivery of information to the media by the press officer.

The press officer should maintain contact with all media personnel for the duration of the emergency, assure that they remain in approved, safe areas, and issue all pertinent information, in accordance with company policy, as quickly as possible.

The press officer should discuss the text of announcements and releases, and, whenever possible, the answers to questions, with the director of corporate public relations, if there is one.

When the senior executive determines that it is completely

safe, the press office should escort media people to the area in which the emergency occurred and explain the event from the company's perspective.

Safety equipment, such as hard hats, should be readily available and provisions made in advance for distribution to members of the press, as required.

The senior executive should be available for interviews as frequently as possible. In his absence, other company spokespeople should substitute.

Regardless of the amount of coverage made individually by members of the press, the press officer should be constantly gathering facts for the purpose of issuing the company's own releases.

In cases where statements relating to the emergency are made by persons outside the company, such as government officials, the media should be invited to request the company's comments in order to avoid a situation where incorrect information is being made public without challenge.

The same full cooperation, within the requirements of safety, that is accorded to the print media should be given to radio and television representatives.

COMMUNICATIONS WITH OTHER PUBLICS

Depending upon the nature and duration of the emergency, special measures may be required to communicate with employees. Spot announcements on local radio stations, newspaper ads, and telephone calls on an organized basis are devices that may be used. Radio spots might also be used to reassure employees' families, if the emergency occurs during the workday.

If the problem is a severe one, the company might want to contact key community leaders by telephone as quickly as possible so that they have the facts at hand for those who might question them. If such phone contact is necessary, the senior executive should assign specific personnel to make the calls.

All communication with shareholders and members of the financial community is the responsibility of corporate headquarters.

WHEN THE SMOKE CLEARS

A story never ends when the emergency is over. The follow-up can be of great importance.

Stories should be developed and placed regarding the company's efforts in aiding victims, reconstruction, and future safeguards. Actions to thank the community for its help and other activities that demonstrate the company's concern for its employees and the public should be included as well.

A letter to employees reassuring them about future operations might be valuable.

You might send positive follow-up material to your list of community leaders and organizations. The same or a similar mailing might go to your lists of customers and suppliers.

Material might be provided to corporate headquarters for distribution to shareholders and members of the financial community.

Immediately after the emergency, it is advisable for the unit's public-relations executive to discuss with corporate headquarters a complete and well-coordinated follow-up program.

7

THE ELEMENTS OF A PUBLIC-RELATIONS PROGRAM: THE SHAREHOLDERS, FINANCIAL COMMUNITY, AND OTHER PUBLICS

There are a number of other publics and techniques that may not be as visible as those already discussed but that must, nonetheless, be a part of any total communications effort. This chapter will cover the development of relationships with special publics, such as shareholders and the financial community, and will explore several additional public-relations techniques, including direct-mail communications and person-to-person contacts between company and community members.

SHAREHOLDER RELATIONS

While the shareholders comprise an extremely important audience for the overall company public-relations effort, unless you are a corporate public-relations executive you will probably be less active in this area.

In most publicly held companies, maintaining and improving relations with shareholders is the responsibility of the corporate public-relations staff. The annual report, quarterly reports, special reports, and meetings are all part of this effort.

If you are a line officer, your primary responsibility will be to help establish the performance upon which this phase of the program is based. It is your job, as well, to communicate that performance accurately to corporate headquarters so that it can be utilized in the total effort.

As we mentioned in the section "A Nose for News" (page 8),

activities that are routine to you may be of great interest to people unfamiliar with your operation. Pass such items along to corporate headquarters for dissemination to stockholders.

Obviously, letters, phone calls, or visits from shareholders should be treated as if they were from your bosses. In a sense, they are. Of course you will be courteous. In addition, be cautious. Be aware of what information you should not reveal without prior approval from headquarters.

If you do not know the answer to a question or if you think the requested information is outside your area of responsibility, refer the stockholder to the proper corporate executive. When in doubt, do not commit yourself. This is not withholding information, but it is, rather, an attempt to give out correct information at the proper time.

FINANCIAL-COMMUNITY AND INVESTOR RELATIONS

Basically what we have said about the shareholders pertains to the financial community at large and to potential investors. A corporate public-relations department communicates with this public through meetings with security analysts, bankers, brokers, investment bankers, and via contacts with the financial services, regular mailings, personal discussions, and other methods.

The chief responsibility of the line officer is to communicate results to corporate headquarters.

Of course, any financial or investment consultant who contacts you may possess the power to make a significant difference to the well-being of the company. He or she should be treated with the same courtesy—and caution—as a shareholder. To repeat: When in doubt, say nothing.

EMPLOYEE RELATIONS

It has become an accepted fact of business life that a company is as good as the people who work for it. Their skills, attitudes, and dedication create the corporate personality.

The principal motivation for any worker is the compensation that he or she receives. It would be naive to deny this. However, in our complex society, many elements other than a paycheck influence employee attitudes. These might include working conditions, recognition by the management, peer approval, personal involvement in decision-making, and the conception that the individual has formed about his or her own relationship to the company.

Specifics of employee relations vary with each company, but every member of management, both staff and line, can contribute to this important part of the program.

CUSTOMER RELATIONS

No wheels turn, no factory works, no goods are distributed, no profits are earned or dividends paid until a sale is made. The most important single individual to any company is the person who makes that sale possible—the customer. On his or her shoulders rests the entire corporate superstructure. Without the customer, there is no company.

Customer relations must permeate every phase of the public-relations program as well as every phase of corporate life. From the worker in the mine or factory, through the salespeople and management staff, to the chairman and president, the customer must be the "main man."

All the techniques outlined in this book, all the activities suggested, have, as the final public, that customer.

You, as a public-relations officer for your company, have the most complete knowledge of your primary customers. They serve the ultimate consumer you wish to reach. You know if you sell to dealers, retailers, wholesalers, or jobbers. You know where they are located and what their position is in the industry. In short, you know who your customers are.

However, it might be advantageous to clarify your relationship with them in your own mind and to assess in what ways that relationship can be improved. Determine, once more, which of them has the possibility of becoming a more important purchaser. Consider, again, potential new customers—those people to whom you *should* be selling. If you have not already done so, list all present customers, indicating those who should be more active, and then list, as well, firms that might become customers. (You probably already have such lists. Make sure that they are current.)

This does not presume to suggest sales approaches. That is not our area of expertise. But public relations can reinforce your company's sales effort to make the prospect a customer and the moderate purchaser an important one.

INDUSTRY AND TRADE RELATIONS

The industry in which your company functions is your immediate family. Among its members are your primary customers, your suppliers, and your competitors. These people are your peers, and their view of your company will do much to influence a broader public and will play a part in the atmosphere in which you do business.

Your company should keep the trade press informed of its activities, participate in industry associations, and sit in on their decision-making councils, establish itself as a leading spokesman for the industry's needs and objectives, and, in general, play a significant role in its prosperity.

Frequently, an individual company's public-relations program will be directed to the promotion of the industry as a whole. Activities will be initiated in which the company name or its products are not even mentioned. Management should be aware that when the industry prospers, the company will benefit by capturing its fair share of the new markets opened and current ones expanded.

SALES PROMOTION AND POINT-OF-SALES

Sales promotion cannot be dealt with effectively in general terms. It can include contests, giveaways, awards, tie-ins, window displays, and many other special projects.

In addition, if your company has its own retail outlets or supplies others directly, point-of-sales promotion is an important part of its public-relations effort. Obviously, a person who enters an establishment for any purpose is the best potential customer.

The attractiveness of the displays, the completeness of the lines, the interest created, and the attitude and knowledge of the sales personnel can convert a shopper into a buyer or a small purchaser into a large one.

This will have particular application to those departments that concentrate on the consumer.

PERSONAL CONTACTS

When an executive of any company enters a social situation, he or she is a representative of that company, like it or not. Presuming normal, friendly behavior, the reflection on that firm will be favorable. But the executive can accomplish more than that.

Americans are interested in what other people do for a living. In very few other countries around the world would a newly met acquaintance ask, "What do you do?" or "What business are you in?" In the United States this is accepted social behavior. A company executive should be equipped to answer—to really *tell*—the interested questioner what the company does, makes, and sells. This is an effective and inexpensive way to acquaint a broad audience with the company's story. Of course, the more friends the executive makes in varied circles, the broader that audience will be.

DIRECT MAIL

Direct mail is a well-accepted communications tool that must be carefully and conservatively used. Not only is it very expensive, but also it must be expertly prepared or it will end up in innumerable wastebaskets.

Any company must consider in great detail to whom it will send direct mail. Each piece must be targeted to a specific audience and the response must be carefully monitored and analyzed.

Coordination with all levels of management, including corporate, is essential in this phase of the operation, as in all others.

MERCHANDISING RESULTS

The impact of a story in a newspaper or magazine, an interview on radio or television, a particularly effective ad, an impressive direct-mail piece, a speech before a group or club—all these communications accomplishments can be multiplied many times over if they are merchandised properly.

A company should reprint montages of magazine and newspaper stories that have appeared, texts of speeches and interviews, advertisements, and other pertinent material, and send them to customers, shareholders, and other interested parties. It should use them for point-of-sale displays and in kits for its salespeople.

What others say about a company has a ring of authenticity that nothing it says about itself can equal.

8

THE SPEAKERS' BUREAU

In planning a complete communications program, the public-relations executive must determine who is available to appear on television or radio, who can be interviewed by the trade and consumer press, or who can speak to organizations whose memberships are important to the firm.

He or she must look for people who are experts in a particular field, even if it is only remotely connected with the company's business. A toy manufacturer might have a child psychologist on staff; a food company, a qualified nutritionist; an electronics firm, a specialist in that field.

The public-relations executive should always be interested in arranging speaking engagements and personal appearances for company representatives, even if nothing is mentioned about the company's products or services. The fact that the representative is introduced as vice-president of the company, and then speaks with expertise and knowledge, has great value. The demonstrated competence of the speaker is transferred to the company in the mind of the listener, viewer, or reader.

In addition, a public appearance by a company executive is the launching pad for attendant publicity: releases to the media; announcements to customers, shareholders, and the financial community when appropriate; and follow-up reprints of the speech or interview are all effective. If properly used, this phase of the program can be extremely productive at a relatively low cost.

Certain people in your unit might be qualified to handle such general topics as energy sources, ecology, or good corporate citizenship. Others will be more effective in specific areas of expertise.

The first step in creating your speakers' bureau is the compilation of a card file of speakers, even if you have only two or three available. This file should list each speaker separately and include name, biographical data, subject or subjects the speaker can discuss, record of speeches made, and, to the extent possible, reaction to those speeches. This file will be used in selecting speakers for specific audiences and in maintaining a running record of accomplishments.

The second step is the identification of audiences. Business clubs, chambers of commerce, fraternal organizations, and many other groups are always in need of good speakers for their programs. They usually have program directors—volunteers charged with the responsibility of providing their groups with interesting and stimulating talks. Develop a list of these organizations and their program chairmen in your area, once again by using the phone books and the telephone.

When you have completed your speakers' file and your audience list, you will have set the foundation for a valuable and versatile public-relations tool.

TIPS ON SPEECH-WRITING AND DELIVERY

You have now established a speakers' bureau and are ready to book appearances for yourself or for other executives.

Once an engagement has been scheduled and a topic chosen, either in consultation with the audience group or at their request, the speaker is ready to begin preparation.

In many cases the subject matter will be so familiar that little research will be necessary. No matter how knowledgeable the speaker may be, however, he or she should carefully marshal facts, statistics, and other materials to support the positions he or she intends to take.

After the research has been completed and the required facts and anecdotes assembled, the next step is the preparation of an outline. It is advisable to begin with a rough listing of the points to be covered, then to develop it into a detailed outline, working with the material that has been collected.

THE FINISHED SPEECH

When the outline is completed, two methods can be used in developing the wording of the speech. It may be written word-for-word and read, or it may be spoken extemporaneously, following the outline, without preparing a full written text. The extemporaneous method of presentation gives the speaker more flexibility and permits more spontaneity, but if policy statements are to be made, it may be desirable to prepare a written text to avoid misinterpretations.

Many good public speakers combine these two methods. They prepare a full text and go over it many times until they become very familiar with it. For the actual appearance, however, they use the outline, depending upon their knowledge of the text to give them mental and verbal ease.

A crucial element to be considered in the preparation of the speech is the nature of the audience. Age, sex, and profession of the audience, as well as other demographic factors, must influence both the content and the phraseology of the speech. Technical terms should be avoided unless the group is familiar with them.

In general, use short, uncomplicated sentences. A simple word or phrase is always preferable to long, involved explanations. A speaker should not be interested in displaying erudition. The objective is to inform, educate, and interest the audience. The speech should be just long enough to cover the topic. The material should not be padded.

One of the shortest speeches on record was delivered by Henry Ford at Light's Golden Jubilee in Atlantic City in 1929. The other businessmen and politicians on the platform spent hours extolling the benefits of electricity. When the crowd shouted for Ford he got up and said, "We build at Dearborn eight thousand complete electric-light plants every day. This being an electrical meeting, I thought I'd like to tell you that. Thank you." And he sat down.

Abraham Lincoln's famous address was by far the shortest speech given at Gettysburg on that historic day. Obviously, longer is not necessarily better.

Most of us are not comedians. The old after-dinner speaker's habit of including "jokes" in a speech is obsolete. They are usually strained, inferior jokes that half the audience has heard before. Many speakers have the wit and sense of humor to find amusing aspects in the material itself. This kind of light, informal approach is far superior to the overworked joke. The speaker should not, however, feel an obligation to be "funny." That is Bob Hope's job and he gets paid very well for it.

To sum up, the speech should be brief, simple, and as light and informal as the material permits. It should be well-researched and completely accurate. Remember—the speaker is the voice of the organization.

Whenever possible, the speech should be submitted to corporate public relations or the office of the chief executive officer in advance of presentation. If statements of company policy or company and/or industry positions on national issues are included in the remarks, then this is essential.

THE PRESENTATION

Before going in front of the actual audience the speaker should practice delivering the speech. This should be done alone, aloud, and, ultimately, without script if possible. Even though the outline or the verbatim text will be used by the speaker at the time of the talk, it is essential that he become thoroughly familiar with the material beforehand.

In many cases, it is desirable to enhance a speech with the use of visual aids. These might consist of slides, filmstrips, enlarged photos, charts, drawings on a blackboard, or product samples. These aids should be used only when they serve the purpose of making the presentation more interesting and effective.

The physical appearance of the speaker is very important. All speakers will, of course, be well-groomed. They should have good posture, a confident manner, and be relaxed, warm, and friendly.

The speaker's first task is to establish contact with the audience. It is a good orator's trick never to speak to the whole group, but to single out individuals and speak to them directly, one after another, until as much of the audience as possible feels that he or she has been personally addressed.

The speaker's voice must, of course, be loud enough to be heard throughout the room, but not so loud that the audience would begin to feel harangued. The tone of voice should be conversational, and not pompous or stagey. The speech pattern should be slow and distinct so that every word is heard and understood. The speaker should be careful to avoid a monotone and should allow easy and natural voice shifts as frequently as the material dictates, for interest and emphasis.

The less the speaker has to refer to notes the better, but if a certain statement must be read to ensure accuracy, this should be done openly and obviously without any attempt at concealment. Any visual aids used should be presented so that the entire audience has a clear view.

If questions and answers are to follow the speech, the company representative should be prepared beforehand. He should try to anticipate what might be asked and formulate answers. During this period the speaker should be courteous, positive, confident, and avoid guessing at answers he does not have. Once the presentation is completed, the speaker should be warm, friendly, and appreciative of compliments and expressions of thanks.

From the instant the speaker enters the room until the time he leaves, he must be aware that he is the face, the voice, the representative of the company.

In most instances, the speakers' bureau that you have established will be able to fill requests from organizations in your area. There may be occasions when a speaker is required to discuss a subject about which no one in your unit has expertise. Do not automatically refuse the booking. Consult first with corporate public relations or the office of the chief executive officer—such a person may be available in another unit of the company.

9

THE BASICS OF PUBLIC
RELATIONS AND PUBLICITY

In this chapter you will find summarized the basic rules of public
relations and publicity, distilled from the material presented in
the foregoing chapters. You might find it useful to have it pho-
tocopied so that it can be kept handy for review and easy
reference.

ALWAYS DO THE FOLLOWING THINGS

1. Develop an overview of the whole company or organization
    for which you work. Learn how various elements interrelate.
2. Use the corporate-identity logo, trademark, colors, and
    motto on all possible occasions.
3. Discuss your unit's activities, its product and services, with
    all your publics, within the confines of corporate and division
    restrictions.
4. Work closely with the division staff and corporate public
    relations, if they exist.
5. Use freely all material contained in annual and quarterly
    reports, leaflets, brochures, and other printed material
    published by your company.
6. Be sure all information you use is accurate.
7. Recognize the synergistic connections between your unit,
    your division, all other units and divisions.
8. Call upon corporate public relations, if your company has it,
    for guidance, assistance, material, and ideas when necessary.
    Regard it as your external public-relations agency.
9. Use this check list as a guide for action in all phases of public
    relations.
10. State, but do not try to interpret, company or organization
    policy.

11. Always tell the truth to the media. When in doubt, say nothing.
12. Admit you don't know the answer to a question, if that is the case, and arrange to get the reporter the required information, or refer him or her to someone who can be of help.
13. Be "low key" rather than "hard sell" in your relations with the media.
14. Seek only tasteful, positive publicity.
15. Get to know the media people who are important to your program.
16. Prepare and keep current lists of all the media people with whom you deal.
17. Direct all material to the proper media person.
18. Send all material to media in time to meet deadlines.
19. Include on your media list the trade publications that interest your customers.
20. Promote your unit, its products, and services.
21. Develop a "nose for news."
22. Promote local-media use of press material issued by division headquarters and corporate public relations, if your company has them.
23. Take advantage of the interest created in products by ads to place stories in local media.
24. Show no favorites in the distribution of "hard-news" releases.
25. Keep your word when you give your story exclusively to a reporter.
26. Examine all departments of a publication for feature placement possibilities.
27. Be aware of opportunities in the electronic media.
28. Use the "pitch letter" as a tool.
29. When a feature is turned down, try to place it elsewhere.
30. When a feature is used, rework it with a new angle and try to place it with another publication.
31. Set up editorial interviews whenever possible.
32. Use photography when it will enhance the possibility of a story being used.
33. Be sure that a "cut line" or caption is pasted to the back of every photo you send out.
34. Attempt to place wire-service stories when your material is of broad national interest.

35. Pay special attention to trade papers and magazines.
36. Service the weeklies, shoppers, and club papers in your area.
37. Take advantage of the opportunities presented by the feature services.
38. Be sensitive to issues, specific problems, and economic factors that concern your "affect community."
39. Cooperate in reasonable efforts to protect the environment and to control air, water, and noise pollution and conserve natural resources and the ambiance of the area.
40. Keep local government apprised of your unit's activities and contributions to the community.
41. Encourage community participation in events such as plant openings, tours, and open houses.
42. Communicate your unit's participation in community affairs to the total "affect community."
43. Constantly redefine your "affect community" as your unit's activities broaden.
44. Prepare and keep current a list of all individuals, organizations, and government agencies you wish to inform and educate.
45. Purchase goods and services locally whenever possible.
46. Make sure your unit's facilities are clean, attractive, and that they fit into the surrounding environs.
47. Make a concerted effort to adjust to your community's traffic patterns without disrupting them unduly.
48. Handle all complaints quickly and courteously.
49. Participate in community-service activities and encourage other unit employees to do likewise.
50. Investigate the possibility of your unit's facilities being used in the case of emergencies or disasters.
51. Be at all times a good corporate citizen and a concerned neighbor.
52. Communicate your unit's performance to the division and corporate executives promptly and effectively for inclusion in communications with the company's publics.
53. Treat calls and visits from stockholders or members of the financial community courteously but carefully.
54. Supply stockholders, investors, analysts, and so forth with any information that has been published or approved on the corporate level.

55. Refer to corporate headquarters all questions which you are not able to answer, or requests for information you are not in a position to reveal.
56. Participate in industry groups.
57. Establish your unit's executives (including yourself) as effective spokespeople for your segment of the industry.
58. Participate in activities to further the objectives of the industry even if there appears to be no direct benefit for your company.
59. Keep your primary customers, suppliers, and industry peers informed of your unit's activities.
60. Make your speakers' bureau an active part of your public-relations program.
61. Prepare yourself and other unit executives to be knowledgeable spokespeople even in the course of personal contacts.
62. Merchandise the results of your public-relations efforts.
63. Make suggestions regarding the advertising programs based on your own knowledge and on comments you get from customers, suppliers, and so forth.
64. Alert sales personnel, customers, suppliers, employees, and other interested people when a story on your unit is to appear or an executive is to be interviewed on radio or television.
65. Be equipped to interpret and explain employee benefits.
66. Establish a reputation as a fair and concerned representative of management in your relations with your unit's employees.
67. Make yourself available, within the limitations of your work schedule, to listen to employee grievances that are outside the regular structure.
68. Cooperate in the gathering and preparation of material for the internal house organ, if you have one.
69. Use the house organ as an important employee-relations tool.

DO NOT DO THE FOLLOWING

1. Do not comment on political or economic issues except within the bounds of published or stated company positions.

2. Do not disclose corporate figures, divisional results, or other such information unless it has already been released or unless you have prior approval from corporate headquarters.
3. Do not comment on corporate activity of the company without corporate approval.
4. Do not presume, comment on, or explain any position of the company relative to laws, regulations, economic issues, or government policy.
5. Do not disclose details of internal operations, contents of internal memoranda, advisories, instructions, or other matters.
6. Do not discuss new services, installations, or possible acquisitions without prior clearance from corporate headquarters.
7. Do not discuss matters relating to burglaries, thefts, embezzlements, accidents, disturbances, or other matters (local or corporate) that may have a bearing on the corporate image or that may involve legal questions or insurance claims.
8. Do not discuss company investment policies or philosophies.
9. Do not comment on pending or threatened litigation or other legal proceedings involving your company without prior clearance from corporate headquarters.
10. Do not alter the corporate-identity logo, trademark, colors in any way for any purpose.
11. Do not say anything to a media person anywhere, at any time, on any subject that is "off the record."
12. Do not suggest an exclusive feature to a second reporter before it is definitely refused by the first person you pitched it to.
13. Do not become a pest by calling a publication too frequently to find out if a story has been accepted.
14. Do not invent reasons to call an editor or reporter.
15. Do not pressure a reporter or editor.
16. Do not mention that your company "advertises in the paper."
17. Do not insist on name identification in a story—no matter what its content.
18. Do not ask a reporter if he is going to use a story. It is not his decision.

19. Do not ask to read a story before it is used.
20. Do not send out a story you know to be dull or unimportant or a picture you know to be bad.
21. Do not attempt to service the financial news wires (Dow-Jones and Reuters) without coordinating your efforts with corporate public relations, if it exists in your company.
22. Do not schedule press conferences in any but the most unusual circumstances and then only after prior discussion with the office of the chief executive officer.
23. Do not call a reporter or editor when he or she is on deadline unless you have important news developments.
24. Do not use fee-charging services such as public relations news wires; mat services; feature, news, or picture services; or public-relations mailing houses without prior discussion with corporate headquarters.
25. Do not make any statement to government or community agencies regarding corporate positions or activities unless previously published.
26. Do not take stands on local issues without prior approval of corporate headquarters.
27. Do not make promises of financial or other types of aid on behalf of your unit, division, or company without prior approval.
28. Do not pledge your unit's facilities for any purpose without prior approval.
29. Do not spread yourself too thin in your community-service activities.
30. Do not make personal commitments you cannot fulfill.
31. Do not give any information to a shareholder or member of the financial community unless it is already public knowledge.
32. Do not seek to communicate directly with or influence shareholders or the financial community.
33. Do not reveal any corporate, division, or unit activity that is not public knowledge either to your industry, employees, or personal contacts.
34. Do not become involved in labor negotiations unless they are your responsibility.
35. Do not become involved in the formal, established grievance procedure in your unit unless that is your responsibility.

36. Do not make any statement, comment, or analysis of corporate or division policy, activity, plans, or philosophy to any individual or group unless the material has already been made public or unless you have prior approval.

=**10**=

A CASE HISTORY:
CREATING A CORPORATE
PUBLIC-RELATIONS PROGRAM

When an organization diversifies by rapid acquisition, it may postpone, because other problems are given greater priority, the development of a central, unified public-relations program.

Such was the case with National Gypsum Company, one of the nation's largest integrated and diversified manufacturers of quality products for the building, construction, and shelter industries. It is listed by *Fortune* as one of the top three hundred firms in the nation.

Until five years ago, this major New York Stock Exchange company had no professional corporate public-relations department. Each operating division had a public-relations officer—in most cases a line executive with other responsibilities—and certain elementary corporate public-relations activities were carried out on a haphazard basis.

A number of communications problems convinced an alert management that this situation required attention, and James W. Thompson was retained as director of corporate public relations (subsequently "advertising" was added to his job definition).

Thompson is a "PR pro," having spent many years with big agencies before moving into the corporate area. He had been instrumental in building the strength of the American Express Card while heading up the public-relations department of the credit card and travel-related services divisions of that company.

Upon joining National Gypsum, he organized a department equipped to handle the ordinary day-to-day public-relations requirements effectively. Then, over a period of months, he analyzed the company's basic problems and made his recommendations to management. National Gypsum was suffering an identity crisis but it was not the company itself that was in doubt about who or what it was. It was, most unfortunately, the company's many publics who were unclear about National Gypsum's identity.

Its operating divisions were well known in their particular industries. Its many brand names were "household words" among those who purchased them. Despite this, interviews with top company corporate and division executives produced comments such as:

> "National Gypsum needs to be known better by three audiences—the financial community, our employees, and stockholders."
>
> "Our stock is undervalued."
>
> "There's a general lack of understanding of the company's structure."
>
> "National Gypsum is not a well-understood company—we're involved in much more than gypsum wallboard."
>
> "We need to tell people what National Gypsum is."
>
> "We want to create a positive image for the corporation and for its divisions."

On the other hand, the financial community had known the name of National Gypsum (and its predecessor company) for many years, but a survey of key security analysts in New York made by Thompson revealed great confusion. Comments such as these were made:

> "National Gypsum's primary business is known. It is grouped with U.S. Gypsum, Johns-Manville, and other building-related companies."
>
> "When compared to U.S. Gypsum, National Gypsum is second."
>
> "We are aware that National Gypsum is involved in several different aspects of housing, but we really don't know what they are."
>
> "The company's financial position appears to be good. It's a stable dividend payer."
>
> "National Gypsum doesn't seem to care much about the financial community or about the image it creates among security analysts."

There were other problems related to the lack of a corporate identity. The company and its divisions had not properly positioned themselves in the industries in which they functioned. Its executives had not assumed the leadership roles for which they were qualified and which circumstances demanded of them. In addition, corporate management was convinced that American business in general had not told its story to the people effectively, that it had not properly understood and utilized the media. They felt that every important company was obligated to contribute to the proper understanding of business in the public mind.

THE OBJECTIVES

These, then, were the objectives of the program the new director presented to management:

1. To create a synergistic relationship between National Gypsum's corporate whole and its many parts (divisions and product lines);
2. To improve awareness of the company's unique corporate structure among shareholders, employees, customers, and the financial community;
3. To improve the company's standing in the financial community;
4. To develop a reputation of corporate excellence with the general public and the construction industry, reinforcing the high-quality image of the company's products;
5. To build awareness among employees in all divisions and at all facilities of the nature and scope of the entire corporation;
6. To position the company properly within the many industries in which it functions;
7. To encourage company executives to assume industry leadership status;
8. To make a significant contribution to the American public's understanding of the positive role that business plays in our society.

After management agreed with these objectives and approved budgets to accomplish them, National Gypsum's first coherent, integrated corporate public-relations program was initiated at the beginning of 1978.

THE CORPORATE IDENTITY PROGRAM

The cornerstone of the corporate identity program is an identification system that combines graphics, typography, and color to create a strong connection between the corporate whole and its operating divisions and brand names.

It uses a row of three rhomboids of declining width (one red, one gold, and one black), followed by the name of the division or product in a uniform style of italic boldface on the right and with a phrase such as "A National Gypsum Company" in the same, but much smaller, type below. This identification system is used in all visual areas of communication. The basic graphics, modified to meet specific needs, appear on all the company's printed matter, vehicles, installations—wherever the face of National Gypsum is seen.

The identification system was reinforced by an extensive publicity program directed to the nation's business and financial press, major metropolitan dailies, wire services, local papers in plant cities, trade publications, weeklies, and shoppers, as well as the electronic media, when feasible. Interviews were arranged with major media.

In order to strengthen the program, a special press kit was prepared by the corporate public-relations department and sent to the executive responsible for public relations in all divisions.

The press kit contained:

1. A basic news story on the corporate identity program. In each kit the story was rewritten to feature the particular division to which it was sent.
2. Samples of the identification system—copies of logos, stationery, and so forth.
3. Pictures of installations, facilities, equipment, or vehicles that had been redesigned using the corporate identification motif.
4. A short, light history of the company. This was prepared so that each division could extrapolate the section that had to do with its own history and use it separately.

THE ADDITION OF ADVERTISING

Management was made aware by the new director that advertising was an important element in any total public-relations effort. Its use would permit the company to tell its story to chosen and guaranteed publics in exactly the way it desired.

A number of advertising agencies were invited to present campaigns and budgets designed to support the corporate identity program and other company objectives. Bozell & Jacobs, a national agency with a major presence in Dallas, Texas, where National Gypsum is headquartered, was chosen. Four ads were created for that first year which featured the products of a single division combined with the earnings of the whole company, thereby reinforcing the connection between them. The new corporate logo coupled with the positioning line, "A Family of Companies Building for the Future," cemented each ad together.

The ads began running in September 1978 in the *Wall Street Journal, Businessweek, Forbes, Barron's,* and the *New York Times.* They were scheduled so that the heaviest exposure coincided with the state-of-earnings news release, approximately thirty days after the end of the third fiscal quarter. This increased the impact at a time when it could do the most good for the company.

THE FINANCIAL COMMUNITY

For the first time in National Gypsum's history an integrated financial-community-relations program was instituted.

Meetings were scheduled with several important groups of construction-industry-oriented security analysts, brokers, and other interested people. The chairman, president, and financial vice-president of National Gypsum made presentations. These meetings were designed to further clarify the nature, structure, and strength of the company.

ATTENDANT ACTIVITIES

During that year, the company's top and middle management were involved in the program through meetings, memos, and other material calculated to keep them informed and to elicit their cooperation.

Shareholders received news of the identification program through the quarterly reports and other forms of direct communication.

Speeches to community groups were scheduled for corporate and division executives. These appearances emphasized the relationship of the specific division to National Gypsum.

Division salespeople and representatives carried corporate identification material with them and educated customers, suppliers, and other contacts about the relationship between their divisions and National Gypsum.

FIRST-YEAR RESULTS

Research conducted by an independent firm revealed that the corporate public-relations program had been very well received by the selected test group of security analysts.

The survey indicated that:

- the financial information in the news releases and ads had been useful in helping its various publics to make informed judgments about the company;
- the program had generated enough interest on the part of many analysts to convince them to investigate the company further;
- the program had been effective in helping the public to differentiate among National Gypsum and U.S. Gypsum and other, less diversified building-materials companies.

Requests for annual reports increased from three to fifteen daily. Less formal surveys of customers, suppliers, shareholders, employees, and community groups indicated similar positive results.

THE PROGRAM DEVELOPS

In 1979, the identification system was firmly in place. The publicity campaign was intensified. Two ads were added to the original four so that all divisions were covered. Production figures were updated and dividend increases used instead of earnings figures. Again, the heaviest concentration of ads was scheduled to appear thirty days after the end of each fiscal quarter.

A booklet entitled *Advertising for Growth* was prepared and distributed to all National Gypsum employees. It included copies of the ads and an explanation of the objectives of the corporate identity program and its significance to the individual worker.

The quarterly reports contained a great deal of information about the activities of the operating divisions. This was clearly related to the overall performance of the company.

The results of the second year's efforts were even more encouraging than the previous year's. Another independent survey, conducted in August 1979, revealed:

- awareness among business and financial analysts of National Gypsum increased by 58 percent
- awareness of National Gypsum increased more than twice as much as awareness of the nearest competitor
- National Gypsum came to be regarded as "recession-proof," unlike other companies in the building industry whose fates were linked closely to new housing starts. This was because of the emphasis the public-relations program had put on National Gypsum's penetration of the $80 billion repair and remodeling market.

Once again, all indications were that the company's other publics agreed with the security analysts' perceptions. There were nearly 9,000 requests for annual reports in 1979, up from 3,900 in the previous year, the increase directly attributable to the public-relations program. Accepted research demonstrates that 12 percent of requests of this type result in new shareholders. It can be assumed, then, that the public-relations program created 1,080 new stockholders for the company in that year.

Supporting the survey, 1979 financial results revealed that the company had again reached record levels in both sales and earnings.

WHAT WAS DONE FOR AN ENCORE

In 1980, it was determined to enlist greater participation of division-level executives in the program. The company's first public-relations manual was written and distributed to all division personnel from managers up.

The comprehensive, loose-leaf-bound, 84-page, 8½-by-11-inch manual was given weight by the inclusion of introductory remarks by company president John P. Hayes, and company chairman Robert E. Scifres, indicating their firm belief in the importance of public relations. Its six chapters and six appendixes deal with more than a hundred topics and establish National Gypsum policy in all areas. The manual was introduced at a series of high-level meetings and there has been consistent follow-up to assure that it is being properly utilized.

Reaction from division executives was positive and included comments such as:

"We have needed such a manual for years."
"All the public-relations questions are answered—truly an outstanding publication."
"It is comprehensive, understandable, and yet enjoyable to read."
"My congratulations on a job well done."

The thrust of this phase of the program was to encourage qualified division executives to assume industry leadership positions, to accept speaking engagements, interviews, and other public appearances, to constantly reinforce the relationship between the divisions and the parent company through their activities.

While the public-relations activity generally shifted to the division level, one aspect, the corporate advertising program, was expanded and intensified with a whole new series of ads.

Requests for the annual report in 1980 increased 36 percent over the 1979 figure, to an impressive 11,616. And 11 percent of those who made such requests asked to receive material and information about National Gypsum on an ongoing basis—a sure indication that the company was being considered as an investment possibility. Research indicated that awareness of the company, favorable attitudes toward the company, and knowledge of the various divisions had all increased in 1980.

THE EFFORT CONTINUES

Under the headline, "Together, We're National Gypsum Company," the advertising program has been developed to present a more detailed, complex picture of the National Gypsum structure. Another group of ads was prepared under the heading, "What You'd Use to Build a House, National Gypsum Is Using to Build a Company."

The campaign's employee-relations phase gained great impetus with the publication of a professionally written and edited house organ called *People to People*. While the first issue saw the light at the end of 1980, the paper did not reach maturity until the following year. It has been greeted with unanimous enthusiasm by executives and other employees. One of its primary objectives is to make each worker aware of his or her relationship to the parent company as well as to his or her unit or division.

The corporate public-relations department is offering division executives increased aid in carrying out their public-relations responsibilities through speeches, releases, individually tailored stories, consultations, and joint projects.

SUMMARY

National Gypsum Company can list impressive accomplishments since the organization of its corporate public-relations department some five years ago. Briefly, these are:

1. an effective, functioning department where none had existed before;
2. a corporate identity program that has achieved demonstrable results and has gone far toward accomplishing its objectives;
3. a total corporate public-relations effort that embraces shareholders, the financial community, employees, suppliers, the industry, the community, and the general public;
4. a corporate advertising program;
5. a coherent schedule of meetings with security analysts, brokers, and other members of the financial community;
6. the company's first public-relations manual, at last establishing consistent, company-wide policies;
7. a professional employee–house organ.

As a result of these accomplishments, in the past five years:

- requests for annual reports have increased from year to year;
- general awareness of National Gypsum and favorable attitudes toward the company have increased appreciably;
- financial analysts' awareness of the company has grown by 31 percent—this is 41 percent greater than for any of its competitors;
- National Gypsum has dramatically improved its overall performance profile and is considered to be a financially sound company—diverse and well managed, with strong potential for the future. Current financial data confirm this estimate;
- the awareness of the company's divisions by security analysts increased by, variously, 16 to 146 percent, depending upon the specific division;
- the research that provided the above information also indicated a direct correlation between National Gypsum's image and the public-relations message stated through both publicity and advertising.

This case history illustrates many of the points that we have tried to make throughout this book. *Public relations works.* It works in concrete, demonstrable terms. It must be professionally planned and executed. Its objectives must be specific and clear. Time, money, and effort must be invested in a program's implementation—but with these things in place, *public relations works dramatically and impressively.*

11

A CASE HISTORY:
A SERIOUS PROBLEM—
A SIMPLE SOLUTION

There is a public-relations legend whose hero varies according to the raconteur. The authors have it on good authority that it was Ben Sonnenberg, one of the creators of the public-relations craft as we know it today.

Some fifty years ago, a major food processor was having a serious marketing problem. The company was canning tuna fish and couldn't sell it. It was excellent tuna, but it was white. At that time, all other brands on the market were pink and the public appeared unwilling to accept the variation.

Ben Sonnenberg was called in by the board of directors to discuss the problem. "Gentlemen," he said, "I will consider it for a week and meet with you again. If I can't help you, you will owe me nothing. However, if I come up with a solution, my fee is one hundred and fifty thousand dollars."

And that was real preinflation money.

The board gulped, agonized, and agreed.

At the meeting a week later, Sonnenberg reported: "I have the solution. From now on, every can of tuna you produce, every ad you place, every display you create, wherever your tuna is seen, sold, or discussed, you will feature the single line—'Guaranteed not to turn pink in the can.'"

This is but one of the many examples of how a simple public-relations idea has changed an entire industry.

12

A CASE HISTORY: MICKEY MOUSE PLANS AHEAD

When Disneyland moved into Anaheim, California, in the early 1960s the city's population was 33,000, and an estimated 270,000 people lived in surrounding Orange County. Of course, both figures have multiplied since then, but at the time it was as if Gulliver had set up housekeeping in Lilliput.

Disney's public-relations people recognized that problems with the community might well arise and they determined to move quickly in an attempt to avoid or minimize them. They instituted two major programs.

The first they called the "Awards Program." Anaheim and Orange County were growing rapidly, not only because of the amusement park. That growth had started before the park moved in. The neighbors that Disney found when they moved in were hard-working, individualistic, but with a great deal of community spirit and pride. The "old-timers" were rapidly converting the newcomers to their way of life and thinking, but there was an obvious need for the expansion and establishment of many community services and facilities.

The Disney organization decided to give recognition to the many people who had been there before them, and to the organizations in the area capable of joining in community projects and making each city in the county a little better.

Each year, Disneyland had six people from the county act as judges who reviewed applications for the funding of various community-service projects. Disney did not monitor the selections, they simply put up the money to finance the chosen projects. The program broadened Disneyland's local image and won the respect of the communities in the county.

In addition, the Disney public-relations department did an intensive educational job, which they labeled "indoctrination program for opinion leaders." In the early days, a study revealed that the annual gross income of the park was about $30 million. The "throw-off" for the area—money spent by visitors for food, lodging, gas, and other items—amounted to about $190 million. This was money that would not have been spent had Disneyland not been there. Over the years, of course, both figures have increased substantially and fluctuated, but the ratio is still probably fairly constant.

Using these facts as a basis, the Disney public-relations department mounted an information campaign that was successful in convincing community leaders to accept the fact that entertainment is an industry subject to the vicissitudes and variations of all industries, and that it provides a very stable income to the city and the county and is worthy of the support of the community.

Despite the most effective community-relations work, problems are bound to occur. Early in Disneyland's history, a group proposed building a twenty-two-story structure immediately north of the park. At night, the building would have been clearly visible from "Frontierland," completely destroying the illusion that Disney had spent millions to create. After many meetings and discussions, the project was scaled down to fourteen stories, which could not be seen from the park. More important, Disney won the adoption of a land-use policy that recognized the idea of intrusion on illusion—the first such policy ever established, so far as we know.

This is a classic example of how a strong existing community-relations program can be of inestimable help to any company, at any time, in the event that problems should arise.

13

A CASE HISTORY:
THE RESTYLING OF AN IMAGE

Brooke Shields would not be cavorting seductively on TV today, there would be no catchy blue-jean jingles—in fact, there would be no designer-jean industry—were it not for the work of a trade association, a public-relations agency, and an imaginative account supervisor and his team, over twenty-five years ago.

In September 1957, Buffalo, New York, passed an edict banning the wearing of blue jeans to high schools in the area. The "Buffalo Plan" soon spread to school districts throughout the United States.

Around that time someone had written a play, which made it to Broadway and which dealt with the subject of juvenile delinquency. The play was called *Blue Denim*. A newspaper complained that, "Youngsters who are completely neglectful of their appearance are wearing sloppy jackets and worn-out dungarees."

In the public eye, blue jeans meant youthful crime, sloppiness, and teenage rebellion. Yet, by 1963, that image had been completely changed. Princess Anne of England was photographed wearing blue jeans; they were accepted and popular on college campuses, and they were worn by the Peace Corps and other "wholesome" young people. In addition, denim had begun to be used as a fashion fabric.

The story behind the change began in 1956 when the ten biggest producers of the fabric formed themselves into the Denim Council. They were alarmed at the lack of demand for denim and blue jeans, particularly since the peak postwar year of 1953. Their original objective was to put school children back in blue jeans through a concerted national public-relations, advertising, and promotional effort.

The council started to appeal directly to students with a weekly *Teenage Jeanletter*, teenage citizen awards, and other techniques to maintain the goodwill that the young people held for their blue jeans.

It soon became apparent that the problem was not with the teenagers, who had never really been "turned off" their jeans. As successful as these programs were, and as much as the students cooperated, they did not change the minds of the boards of education and the PTAs who had instituted the bans. In addition, the denim industry was consistently losing ground in the adult market. Denim for work wear, leisure, and boys' wear was losing business to other fabrics.

Early in 1960, the mills took an agonizing look at the Denim Council program and determined that a drastic change of direction was needed. They selected Robert S. Taplinger Associates, a public-relations agency, to determine and direct that change. Robert McLaren, the agency's executive vice-president at the time, became account supervisor. He assembled a top team consisting of an account executive, a fashion coordinator, media-placement experts, writers, and other specialists in various phases of public relations.

McLaren directed a survey of retailers, manufacturers, and jobbers in order to obtain their viewpoint on the sale of denim garments. The answers confirmed that there was an ongoing and steady decline in public demand and indicated, as well, a lack of style-merchandising as one of the negative factors.

The McLaren team reasoned that the public image of the durable, hundred-year-old fabric had been influenced by the juvenile-delinquency label to the point where mothers were not buying denim garments for their families or for themselves, the mass psychology being that the wearing of blue jeans automatically made one a delinquent.

Upgrading the fabric's image involved reselling the most important element in the market—women. McLaren's fashion people began an intensive missionary push with the leading designers in the sportswear field. By selling the durability and versatility of the fabric, the team was able to overcome a great deal of hesitancy on the part of the fashion designers and prevailed upon them to produce the first new styles in denim women's wear in years.

Then, using photographs of the new designs, the agency embarked on an intensive publicity push through newspapers, magazines, and other national media. Media reluctance was overcome by pitching to the women's editors of several major publications and wire services with the innovative concept in sportswear and the "new look" of the garments.

These designs were put into production by the force of popular demand and were an instant success. By fall of 1960, ski clothes of denim lined with Dynel appeared. Spring of 1961 saw almost all the major sportswear designers including a number of denim garments in their lines. Such designers as John Weitz and Bonnie Cashin produced complete denim boating lines.

The designer swing to denim, and the consumers' acceptance, was such that the manufacturers were overwhelmed with orders. McLaren was an old pro, however. He did not permit his team to rest on its success. He recognized that momentum, once gained, should never be allowed to fizzle.

A cartoon feature entitled *Denim Men of America* was distributed to media nationally; at the retail level, a "National Denim Days" campaign (later changed to "Fall Denim Days") was initiated and other activity was maintained.

At this point, some of the mills that were members of the Denim Council were confused. They saw the primary objective of the program as upgrading blue denim and selling blue jeans and work wear, not fashion garments for women. The McLaren team was way ahead of them. They enlisted the aid of seventeen of the nation's foremost sportswear designers to provide original designs in men's and women's work and utility clothing. These were presented at a large press breakfast at a New York restaurant early in January 1961, and they received impressive editorial attention from almost every important newspaper and magazine in the country.

McLaren, who was deeply involved in financial-community relations with his other accounts, then pulled a coup they still talk about on Wall Street. At an afternoon cocktail party (after the market closed) he presented the same fashion show to a group of security analysts and business reporters who covered the denim industry. They were delighted at the innovative approach, so different from the dry financial speeches to which they were usually exposed, and showed new interest in the securities of the mills that were members of the council.

Stories were prepared for the menswear publications emphasizing the comfort and good looks of denim sportswear and work wear. A series of articles with pictures, called "A Boy's Life," was released through the major syndicates, comparing the activities of boys today with those of their fathers' time—school, fishing, boating, hunting, and other sports. Of course, the wearing of blue jeans was emphasized throughout. A "Blue Jean Queen" was selected to visit stores throughout America and initiate in-store promotions.

McLaren's team approached the Peace Corps on behalf of the council with an offer of jeans for an entire Peace Corps contingent. The corps officials selected jumper-style culottes for women, jeans for men, plus shorts, blouses, and jackets. Within months the initial two hundred Peace Corps members were completely outfitted in denim. The Denim Council's gift received national publicity.

The activity on behalf of the industry continued. Sales went up. The juvenile delinquent stigma was completely erased. Blue jeans became a status symbol. The rest, as public speakers like to say, is history. No one can watch television or read a paper or magazine today without recognizing the importance of blue jeans and denim generally.

The story of the Denim Council, Robert S. Taplinger Associates, and Robert McLaren and his highly skilled team is a classic instance of public relations not only resurrecting but reshaping an entire industry.

14

A CASE HISTORY:
THE CASE FOR THE
ROSE-COLORED GLASSES

Several of the case histories in this book have illustrated how a constructive public-relations program has changed or created an industry. This is another such example.

Today, sunglasses are a part of every woman's fashion wardrobe—and many a man's as well. Most of us have several different pairs in various shapes and colors. Their price is within our budgets. It was not always thus. "Good" sunglasses were once the luxury of movie stars and rich folks.

World War II created a huge demand for sunglasses by the military—a demand so substantial that the traditional manufacturers of sunglasses, suppliers to the optical trade, could not meet it.

The armed services turned to a small group of plastics companies that were supplying inexpensive sunglasses to the variety chains and drugstores. They were inexpensive because the frames were mass-produced by injection molding. The lenses were made from "drawn" sheet glass, which, after cutting, was formed into a convex shape after being dropped onto a hot mold. These were called "drawn and dropped" lenses, in contrast to those produced by the optical eyeglass manufacturers, which were ground and polished.

The purpose of grinding and polishing is to prepare eyeglasses according to a prescription, a plus or minus magnification. Ordinary sunglasses do not require these expensive processes to serve their principle function, which is to protect against glare.

After the war a huge, new market for sunglasses opened up. The glamour image of the high-flying pilot or the desert commander in his colored glasses was firmly planted in the American mind and everyone wanted a pair. The battle lines for this new market were drawn.

The conventional optical manufacturers had the initial advantage. The term "ground and polished lenses" had a high-quality image carried over from its use in the prescription-eyeglass field. Many people were willing to pay higher prices to opticians and department stores for this apparent hallmark of quality.

The plastics companies were satisfied to serve the mushrooming demand for low-priced sunglasses that the war had created, but the optical people seemed to fear for their traditional markets. Or perhaps they saw the opportunity to corner the entire market on their own terms. They began to attack the plastics companies' use of drawn and dropped, or molded, lenses in their sunglasses with the assertion that the lenses would hurt the wearer's eyes. Only ground and polished lenses were safe, they said in news releases in daily papers and consumer magazines across the country.

The low-price sunglass industry was in great danger. The L. J. Houze Convex Glass Company of Point Marion, Pennsylvania, made practically all the drawn and dropped lenses for the industry. This was virtually their only product. The ten plastics companies that made the sunglasses themselves had already formed a trade group called the Sunglass Institute, led by the Foster Grant Company, the largest producer at that time.

If the optical industry could make its charges stick, the members of the institute and the Houze Glass Company were in real trouble. The massive production facilities built to serve the armed forces would stand idle. Millions of dollars and thousands of jobs were at stake. Already the adverse publicity, supported by advertising created by the optical industry, was worrying sunglass purchasers in variety chains and discount and drugstores. Customers were questioning store clerks about the issue.

A counterattack was mounted. The Houze Glass Company, with the full support of the members of the Sunglass Institute, went to Hill and Knowlton, one of the nation's most prestigious public-relations firms, for help.

The problem, and the account, was assigned to Samuel S. Tyndall, a group vice-president, and to account executive Robert Paterson. Tyndall decided that the first step toward any solution was to determine if there was any truth in the allegations that the molded lenses hurt the wearer's eyes.

The best technical advice available was from Dr. Robert H. Peckham, an expert in ophthalmological research. In the early

1950s, Dr. Peckham was associated with the Temple University School of Medicine as a researcher in ophthalmology. During the war he had been secretary and researcher for the Army-Navy Vision Committee. He had dealt mainly with the great need for glare protection in many combat situations, including prevention of night blindness. He had advised the members of the Sunglass Institute during the period when they were gearing up to meet the extensive wartime demand. Hill and Knowlton immediately retained Dr. Peckham to investigate the opticians' charges.

The charges boiled down to the contention that, because molded glasses were made from sheet glass, there were "waves" in the lenses which could be seen if they were held at arm's length and moved up and down in the light. There were no such waves in glasses that had been ground and polished.

Dr. Peckham embarked on a series of studies to determine (by testing the eyes of those who wore both types of sunglasses) whether there was any difference in the ability to see through a ground and polished lens or one molded from sheet glass. After hundreds of tests with sensitive optical instruments it was proven that the wearer's visual acuity was the same, no matter which type of glasses were worn.

As Dr. Peckham said, "You don't wear sunglasses at arm's length from your eyes. You wear them on your nose where the minute waves make absolutely no difference in your ability to see." Using this information, plus previously unpublished wartime research indicating the dangers of excessive exposure to glare, Dr. Peckham prepared a series of technical papers. These were circulated to the medical profession—ophthalmologists—first at Temple University and then throughout the country. Dr. Peckham spoke extensively to groups of eye doctors.

The Tyndall-Paterson team quickly translated this technical information into everyday terms. The consumer press was saturated with stories. Two news points were made: the demonstrated need for protection from glare; and the proven fact that there was absolutely no difference in the wearer's ability to see through either type of lens. The clear inference was that the only difference was price.

The campaign was progressing so successfully that in 1952, when Sam Tyndall left to open his own public-relations agency, the account went with him. There, assisted by Gar Schmitt and

Jane Austin Secola, he continued the program. Press conferences were held and fashion shows were staged by the Houze Glass Company with the members of the Sunglass Institute in attendance. Dr. Peckham demonstrated with lights and optical instruments what effect overexposure to the sun had on people's eyes. The propaganda of the optical trade was repudiated and, at the same time, an improved image of inexpensive sunglasses was presented to the media and the public. The message was clear. Everybody needs sunglasses. They are valuable and necessary protection for the eyes, as well as a fashion accessory. Most people cannot afford the prices charged by optical or department stores. The variety chains and drugstores make available to the masses sunglasses that are just as safe and effective as the more expensive kind. This was the theme of the ongoing campaign.

The market for inexpensive glasses was protected. The public-relations program saved Houze Glass Company and helped the members of the Sunglass Institute to develop what is today a $600 million industry.

An indication of the success of the Hill and Knowlton/Samuel S. Tyndall Associates information program could be found in two stories that appeared in the *Reader's Digest* some five years apart. In 1950 the magazine published an article warning readers to beware of cheap sunglasses. In 1955 that same publication ran a story quoting Dr. Peckham as saying it did not make any difference what you paid for sunglasses; the most important consideration was that they be dark enough.

Perhaps the most important proof of the success of this public-relations program can be supplied by you, the reader. When was the last time you asked if sunglass lenses were drawn and dropped or ground and polished?

15

HIGHLIGHTS IN
THE HISTORY OF
PUBLIC RELATIONS

Public relations did not start in 1946, as some people claim. It goes back as far as human communication.

The Romans had their Plutarch; Alexander the Great his Aristotle. The beliefs of Jesus of Nazareth would have remained confined to the small mountainous country of his birth had not St. Paul determined to spread his message.

In England, the Plantagenets, the Tudors, the Stuarts—all had their official "historians" who presented facts to suit the interests of the ruling family. Without a doubt, the greatest public-relations man of his time was William Shakespeare. His completely distorted picture of Richard III, for instance, was created to please Elizabeth I, his monarch and sponsor, whose grandfather, Henry VII, had usurped Richard's throne. Today, only professional historians realize that Richard was not a cripple or a villain, that there is no evidence that he had his nephews or anyone else murdered, and that, had he lived, he would probably have been one of the greatest of England's kings. The rest of us believe the picture that the skilled publicist Shakespeare created.

England was not unique. Richelieu in France, all the popes and Holy Roman Emperors and the other rulers of the Middle Ages, had their court historians and publicists. Many a throne was lost, not to the sword, but to the broadside, gossip, and rumor.

Public relations in the United States started with George Washington. Whenever he wrote a letter he made sure that copies were sent to the local papers. Abraham Lincoln did the same. His attitude toward public relations is expressed in the quote that begins this book. The people who helped Washington, Lincoln, and the presidents in between to get their words into print were not called press secretaries or officers. They were called administrative assistants, but, basically, they were doing a public-relations job.

The first publication devoted to public relations that we have discovered was called *Persuasion* and it was published in England in 1919.

The actual beginnings of modern public relations in this country might well be traced to World War I and a book by Walter Lippmann entitled *Public Opinion,* which lays down the basics of what we now know as the public-relations profession.

George Creel was the first actual full-time propagandist for the United States government. He was in charge of public information during World War I. When it was over, he, Edward Bernays, and other pioneers who had cut their teeth in government service set up their own agencies. They had limited media with which to work and called themselves "counselors," advising their clients on how to get their names into the papers and how to change their public images. The classic examples, of course, are the publicity stunts Ivy Lee pulled off on behalf of old John D. Rockefeller in order to make him more "loveable." Lee's classic, of course, was to have John D. distribute dimes to crowds whenever he appeared. This not only implied generosity in those Depression days, it also guaranteed him a cheering mob wherever he went.

During the first decades of the twentieth century, the railroads and utilities ran wild, casually stomping on the rights of the American people. They hired publicists to make their outlaw tactics palatable. Those of us in the profession today would like to forget that many of these early practitioners bought publicity in newspapers by buying newspapermen. We'd like to forget it, but it is a fact. When Samuel Insull fled to Europe to avoid prosecution, it was revealed that he had more than fifty newspapermen in his home state of Illinois on his payroll.

It is almost unnecessary to point out that this could not happen today. The safeguards built into every newspaper and radio or television network make it impossible for a single reporter, or indeed any group of reporters, to plant false information deliberately. Editors, managing editors, publishers, and copy editors, are all involved in the final news product.

In addition, the public-relations profession has so monitored itself through the Public Relations Society of America, publicity clubs in various cities, and other organizations, that a dishonest practitioner would be quickly exposed.

The pattern of today's public relations began to evolve during World War II with the appointment of Stephen Early as press secretary to President Roosevelt. The creation of the Office of War Information headed by Elmer Davis was another step. Into it were drawn some of the finest writers in the country. The war spawned many of the deans of the public-relations profession. They left the service with a relatively new and marketable skill, opened agencies, and went to work for corporations.

There is little relationship between the naive practice of the 1930s and the complicated, sophisticated public-relations business of the 1980s. On the scene now are public-relations agencies that offer total services; counselors who sit on the boards of directors and do nothing but advise; corporations with staffs of hundreds of public-relations people; advertising agencies with public-relations departments or subsidiaries. There are experts in financial public relations, product publicity, media placement, fashion and technical writing, and perhaps a hundred other specialties.

But all this skilled and competent workforce has a single objective—the same objective George Washington had when he sent copies of his letters to the local newspapers. Public relations then was as it is now: *the total communications effort of a person, a company, an agency, a group, a government, or any organization to its various publics.*

BIBLIOGRAPHY

GENERAL BOOKS ON PUBLIC RELATIONS

Bernays, Edward L. *Crystallizing Public Opinion.* New York: Liveright, 1965.

——.*Engineering of Consent.* 2d ed. Norman, OK: University of Oklahoma Press, 1969.

——.*Public Relations.* Norman, OK: University of Oklahoma Press, 1977.

——.*Your Future in a Public Relations Career.* New York: Rosen Press, 1980.

Blumenthal, L. Roy. *The Practice of Public Relations.* New York: Macmillan, 1972.

Canfield, Bertrand R., and Moore, H. Frazier. *Public Relations Principles, Cases and Problems.* Homewood, IL: Irwin, 1977.

Center, Allen H. *Public Relations Practices: Case Studies.* Englewood Cliffs, NJ: Prentice-Hall, Inc., 1975.

Center, Allen H., and Cutlip, Scott M. *Effective Public Relations.* 5th ed. Englewood Cliffs, NJ: Prentice-Hall, Inc., 1978.

Center, Allen H., and Walsh, Frank E. *Public Relations Practices.* 2d ed. Englewood Cliffs, NJ: Prentice-Hall, Inc., 1981.

Gottlieb, Edward, and Klarnet, Phillip. *Successful Publicity.* New York: Grosset & Dunlap, 1964.

Harris, Morgan, and Karp, Patti. *How to Make News and Influence People.* Blue Ridge Summit, PA: TAB Books, Inc., 1976.

Kuswa, Webster. *Sell Copy.* Cincinnati, OH: Writer's Digest Books, 1979.

Lesly, Phillip. *The People Factor.* Homewood, IL: Irwin, 1974.

——.*How We Communicate.* New York: American Management Association, 1979.

Lewis, Herschell Gordon. *The Businessman's Guide to Advertising and Sales Promotion*. New York: McGraw-Hill, 1974.

———. *How to Handle Your Own Public Relations*. Chicago, IL: Nelson Hall, 1976.

Marston, John E. *Modern Public Relations*. New York: McGraw-Hill, 1979.

Monaghan, Patrick. *Public Relations Careers*. New York: Fairchild, 1972.

Newsom, Doug, and Scott, Alan. *This is PR: The Realities of Public Relations*. Belmont, CA: Wadsworth, 1976.

Nolte, Lawrence W., and Wilcox, Dennis L. *Fundamentals of Public Relations*. 2d ed. New York: Pergamon, 1979.

Reilly, R. *Public Relations in Action*. Englewood Cliffs, NJ: Prentice-Hall, Inc., 1981.

Roalman, Arthur W. *Profitable Public Relations*. Homewood, IL: Irwin, 1968.

Robinson, Edward J. *Public Relations and Survey Research*. New York: Irvington Publishers, 1969.

Ross, Robert Davis. *The Management of Public Relations*. New York: Ronald, 1977.

Simon, Raymond. *Perspectives in Public Relations*. Norman, OK: University of Oklahoma Press, 1966.

———. *Public Relations Management: Cases and Situations*. 2d ed. Columbus, OH: Grid, Inc., 1977.

———. *Publicity and Public Relations Work Text*. Columbus, OH: Grid, Inc., 1978.

———. *Public Relations Concepts and Practices*. 2d ed. Columbus, OH: Grid, Inc., 1980.

Smith, Kenneth Owler. *The Practice of Public Relations: Case Studies by 20 Professionals*. Berkeley: University of California, 1968.

Stanley, Richard E. *Promotions*. Englewood Cliffs, NJ: Prentice-Hall, Inc., 1977.

Steinberg, Charles Side. *The Communicative Arts: An Introduction to Mass Media*. New York: Hastings House Publishers, Inc., 1970.

———. *The Mass Communicators: Public Relations, Public Opinion and Mass Media*. Westport, CT: Greenwood Press, 1973.

———. *The Creation of Consent*. New York: Hastings House Publishers, Inc., 1975.

———. *The Information Establishment: Our Government and the Media*. New York: Hastings House Publishers, Inc., 1980.

———. *Mass Media and Communications.* 2d ed. New York: Hastings House Publishers, Inc., 1972.

Steinberg, Charles Side, and Stanley, Robert H. *The Media Environment.* New York: Hastings House Publishers, Inc., 1976.

Walker, John E. *Public Relations: A Team Effort.* Midland, MI: Pendell, 1976.

Warner, Rawleigh, and Silk, Leonard. *Ideals in Collision.* 2d ed. New York: Columbia University Press, 1978.

Winograd, Gary. *Public Relations.* New York: Museum of Modern Art, 1977.

BOOKS ON BUSINESS AND CORPORATE PUBLIC RELATIONS

Dawe, Jessamon, and Lord, William J. *Functional Business Communication.* 2d ed. Englewood, NJ: Prentice-Hall, Inc., 1974.

Dunn, Samuel Watson. *How Fifteen Transnational Corporations Manage Public Affairs.* Chicago: Crain Books, 1979.

Farley, William E. *Practical Public Relations for the Businessman.* New York: Frederick Fell Publishers, Inc., 1968.

Henry, Kenneth. *Defenders and Shapers of the Corporate Image.* New York: Columbia University Press, 1972.

Olins, Wally. *The Corporate Personality.* New York: Mayflower Books, 1979.

Roalman, Arthur W. *Investor Relations That Work.* New York: American Management Association, 1981.

Selame, Elinor, and Selame, Joe. *Developing a Corporate Identity.* New York: Lebhar Friedman, 1975.

Tedlow, Richard S. *Public Relations and Business: 1900 to 1950.* Rev. ed. Greenwich, CT: Jai Press, 1951.

SOME PUBLIC RELATIONS SPECIALTIES

Bachner, John P. *Public Relations for Nursing Homes.* Springfield, IL: Charles C Thomas, 1974.

Blumenthal, Sid. *The Permanent Campaign.* Boston: Beacon Press, 1980.

Brennan, Jim. *Public Relations Can Be Fun and Easy Especially for Nursing Home People.* Mt. Kisco, NY: Futura Publishing Co., Inc., 1977.

Bronzan, Robert T. *Public Relations, Promotions, and Fund Raising for Athletic and Physical Education Programs.* New York: Wiley, 1977.

Calhoun, Calfrey C. *Public Relations in Secondary School Business Education.* Dallas, TX: Business Publications, Inc., 1960.

Gilbert, William H. *Public Relations in Local Government.* Washington, DC: Internal City Mgmt., 1975.

Hillman, Sheilah. *Public Relations for Private Schools.* Seattle, WA: Hillman Press, 1977.

Kunze, Linda J., and Marchak, John P. *Public Relations Writers.* Educational Research Council of America. Washington, DC: Changing Times, 1974.

Kurtz, H. P. *Public Relations and Fund Raising for Hospitals.* Springfield, IL: Charles C Thomas, 1980.

Marshall, Sol H. *Public Relations Basics for Community Organizations.* Van Nuys, CA: Creative Books Co., 1975.

Marshall, Steven F. *Public Relations for Theatre.* Van Nuys, CA: Creative Books Co., 1980.

Mayer, Frank. *Public Relations for Public School Personnel.* Midland, MI: Pendell, 1974.

Pimlott, J. A. *Public Relations and American Democracy.* Pt. Washington, NY: Kennikat Press Corp., 1971.

Rice, Betty. *Public Relations for Public Libraries.* New York: H.W. Wilson, 1972.

Schmidt, Frances, and Weiner, Harold M. *Public Relations in Health and Welfare.* New York: Columbia University Press, 1960.

Unruh, Adolph, and Willer, Robert A. *Public Relations for Schools.* New York: Pitman, 1974.

Woodress, Fred A. *Public Relations for Community and Junior Colleges.* Danville, IL: Interstate, 1976.

HANDBOOKS, DIRECTORIES, BIBLIOGRAPHIES, AND OTHER INFORMATION VOLUMES (LISTED BY TITLE)

Ayer Directory of Newspapers and Periodicals. Philadelphia: N.W. Ayer & Son, annual.

Bacon's Publicity Checker. Chicago: Bacon's Publishing Co., annual.

College Alumni Publications by Richard Weiner and James F. Colasurdo. New York: Richard Weiner, Inc., 1980.

Dartnell Public Relations Handbook, 2d ed., by Dan Forrestal. Chicago, IL: Dartnell Corp., 1977.

The Family Page Directory. Washington Depot, CT: PR Plus, annual.

Handbook of Practical Public Relations by Alexander B. Adams. New York: Thomas Y. Crowell Co., 1965.

Handbook of Public Relations, 2d ed., by Howard Stephenson. New York: McGraw-Hill, 1971.

Handbook of Special Events for Non-Profit Organizations by Edwin R. Leibert and Bernie E. Sheldon. Chicago: Follett, 1972.

Handbook on International Public Relations. New York: Hill & Knowlton and Knowlton International, 1968.

Investor Relations Handbook by Arthur W. Roalman. New York: American Management Association, 1974.

Lesly's Public Relations Handbook, 2d ed., by Phillip Lesly. Englewood Cliffs, NJ: Prentice-Hall, Inc., 1978.

Metro California Media. Washington Depot, CT: PR Plus, annual.

Military Publications by Richard Weiner. New York: Richard Weiner, Inc., 1979.

New York Publicity Outlets. Washington Depot, CT: PR Plus, annual.

News Bureaus in the United States, 5th ed., by Richard Weiner. New York: Richard Weiner, Inc., 1979.

O'Dwyer's Directory of Corporate Communications. New York: O'Dwyer (J.R.) Company, annual.

O'Dwyer's Directory of Public Relations Executives. New York: O'Dwyer (J.R.) Company, triennial.

O'Dwyer's Directory of Public Relations Firms. New York: O'Dwyer (J.R.) Company, annual.

PR Bluebook. Exeter, NH: P.R. Publishing Co., annual.

Professional's Guide to Public Relations Services, 4th ed., by Richard Weiner. New York: Richard Weiner, Inc., 1980.

Public Relations: A Bibliography by Keith A. Lason. Westwood, MA: F. A. Faxon Co., Inc., 1978.

Public Relations Bibliography, 2d ed., by Scott M. Cutlip. Madison, WI: University of Wisconsin Press, 1965.

Public Relations Handbook by Diane Russell. Midland, MI: Pendell, 1976.

Public Relations Information Sources by Alice Norton. New York: Gale, 1970.

Public Relations Register. New York: Public Relations Society of America (PRSA), annual.

Standard Periodical Directory. New York: Oxbridge Communications, Inc., annual.

Syndicated Columnists by Richard Weiner. New York: Richard Weiner, Inc., 1979.

TV Publicity Outlets—Nationwide. Washington Depot, CT: PR Plus, annual.

Who's Who in Public Relations by Robert L. Barbour. Exeter, NH: P.R. Publishing Co., 1977.

Who's Who in Public Relations (International) by Robert L. Barbour. Exeter, NH: P.R. Publishing Co., 1972.

IMPORTANT PUBLICATIONS IN THE PUBLIC-RELATIONS PROFESSION

Jack O'Dwyer's Newsletter. New York: O'Dwyer (J.R.) Company, weekly.

PUBLICATIONS OF THE PRSA

Public Relations Journal, monthly.
PRSA Newsletter, monthly.
PRSA Channels, monthly.

PR Aids Party Line. New York: PR Aids Periodicals, weekly.
PR Reporter. Exeter, NH: P.R. Publishing Co., weekly.
Practical Public Relations. New York: Current Information Services, Inc., semi-monthly.
Public Relations News. New York: Denny Griswold, weekly.
Public Relations Quarterly. New York: Richard Toohey, quarterly.
Public Relations Review. New York: Communications Research Associates, Inc., quarterly.
Publicist. New York: P.R. Aids Periodicals, bi-monthly.

INDEX

ABOUT THE AUTHORS

MATTHEW J. CULLIGAN has been president of four major corporations, including the Curtis Publishing Company, where in 1963 he orchestrated a massive and successful public-relations campaign that helped to save the company from bankruptcy. During his years as a corporate executive he has worked closely with many public-relations and publicity professionals and has acquired expertise in the field firsthand. Culligan is the author of seven previous books, including *The Curtis-Culligan Story* and *Getting Back to the Basics of Selling.*

DOLPH GREENE has worked in public relations for thirty years and for the past ten has been an independent public-relations/communications consultant. A former executive vice-president of Robert S. Taplinger Associates, a New York City–based public-relations firm, he has also taught public relations at New York University and the New School for Social Research. In 1963 he received the coveted Silver Anvil award of the Public Relations Society of America for outstanding achievement in stockholder relations.